FRICTION SEX

Friction sex is hungry bodies rubbing together. It's lusty, panty-wetting, trouser-tenting - a very physical ache for release.

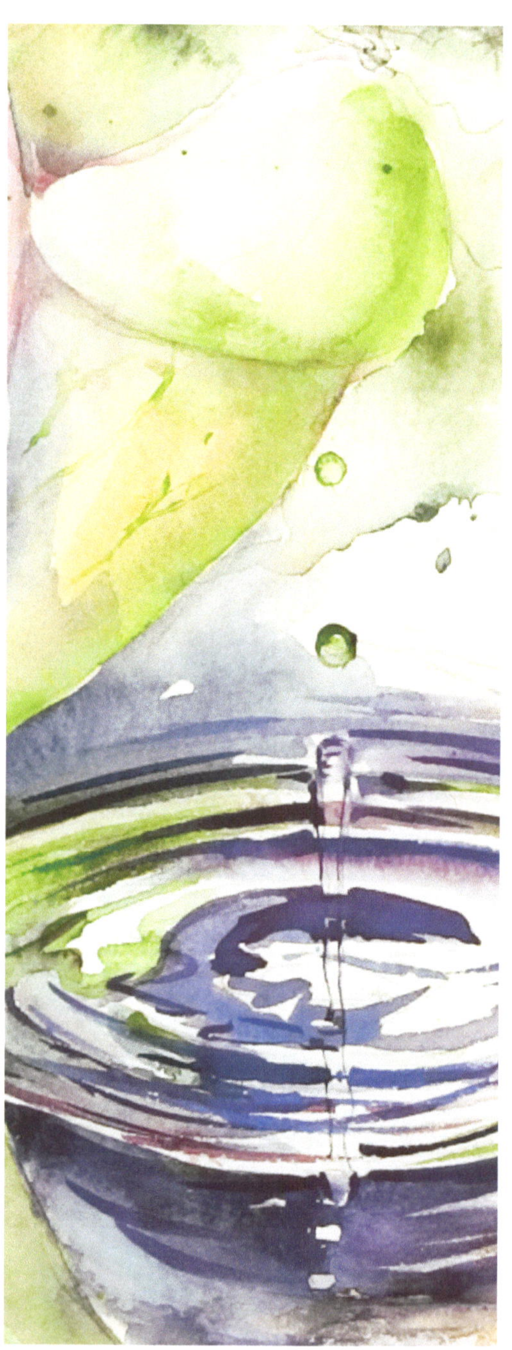

The Power of Song

His Man-ness sings to her
through eyes
ears
tongue
in a voice of honey flame

The song keens her to sweet madness
always she wants him
in her
his silken one-eyed snake
iron head butting against her womb gate
boring a path for the flood

Succor

Sing to me of fruits and trees

Hum a moody melody.
Run your fingers through my hair
and calm the raging fear.

Know that I love you and could never leave,
but don't ever ask me why.
Expect nothing from me, but all that I give
can never be taken away.

Pillow my face between your breasts.
Breathe softly into my ear.
Glance into my soul through the dark pools of
our eyes and whisper "I'll always be here."

Our journey together is down a far road,
the end is nowhere in sight.
We'll fly through the days gladly
and play with each other all night.

Press your fingers around my breasts,
lick my nipples to peaks.
Run your tongue between my toes,
bend over and spread your cheeks.

We'll dance upon the sea,
and in stillness of morning, flooded with light.
We'll laugh and laugh
delectable sounds of delight.

Beg me for pleasure, surrender your charms,
open your door and your gate.
Feel the soft pressure of love's caress
that fills our bodies with heat.

Love me, please love me
with sweetness and warmth,
and sing to me
while I sleep.

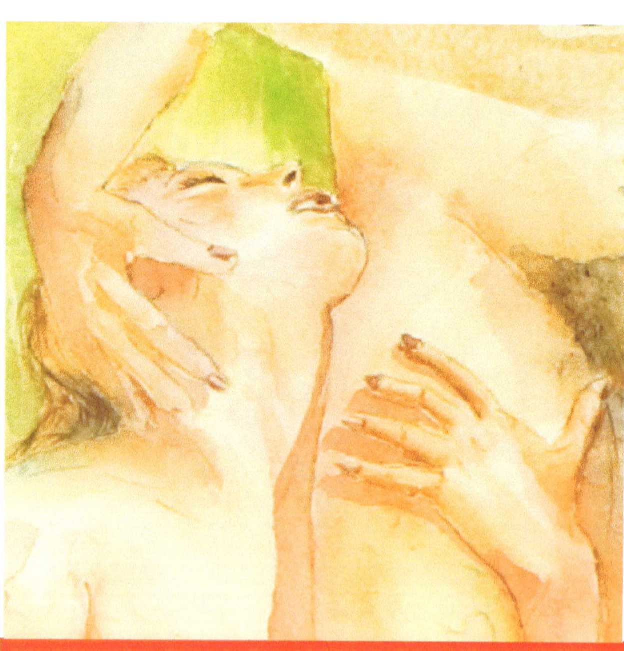

Birthday Song To My Love

I shall sing to my love
with whispers and sighs
I'll entice him
with caresses and moans
I shall lie at his feet
and implore with my eyes
Til my heat scorches through
to his bones

Sunworshippers' Croon

The sun is sizzling
SHE burns hotter

A fire born of wanting
fuelled by knowledge of pleasures past
ecstasy to come

Ripe
Round
Purple
is her flame
her deep scorching brand

His heart steams under its molten kiss

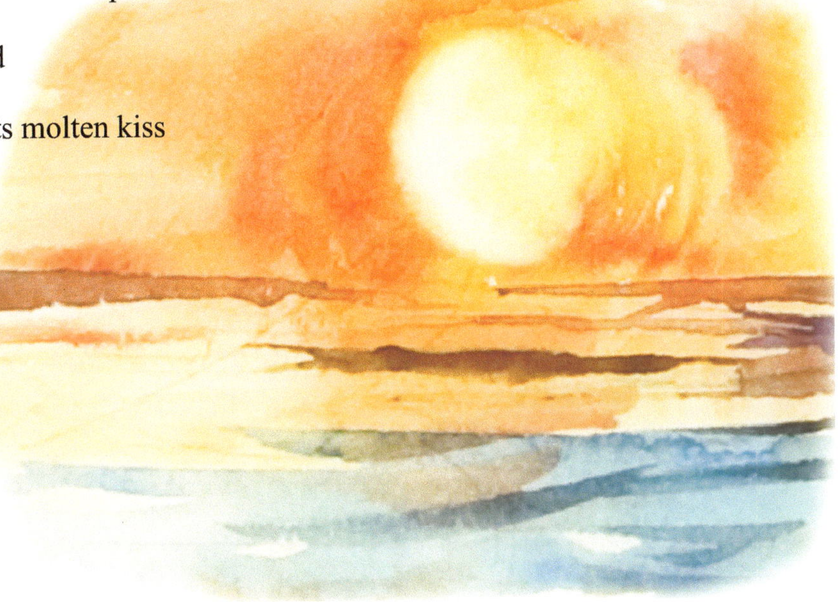

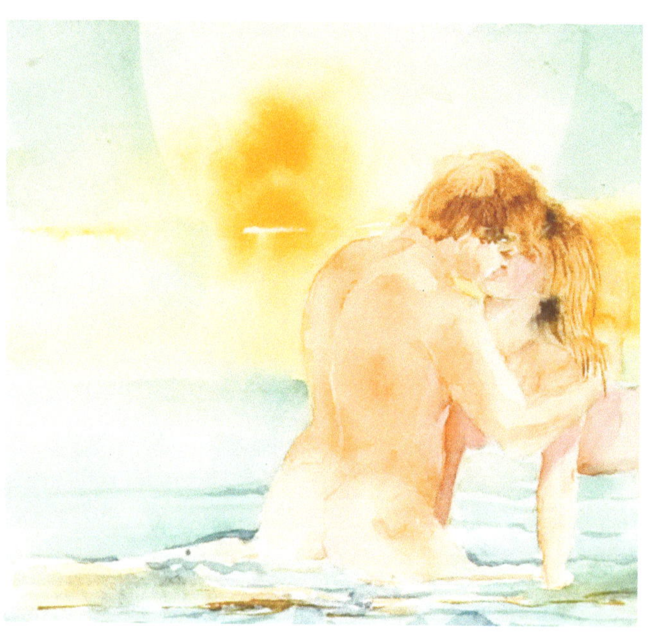

On the Beach

We make
undulations
ripples
rolls
waves
of searing heat

Our tongues speak
Fire
Our loins spew white flame

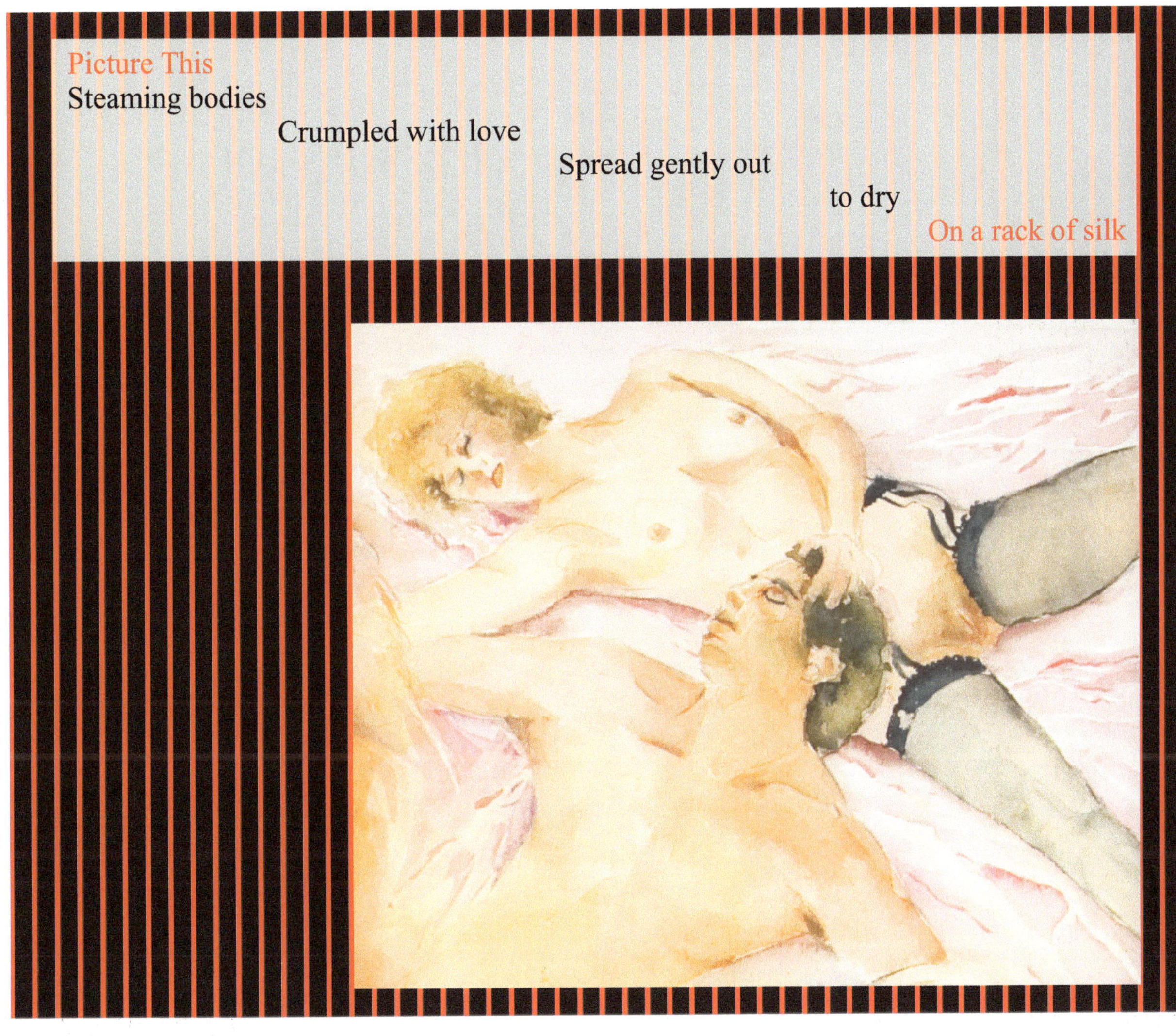
Picture This
Steaming bodies
Crumpled with love
Spread gently out
to dry
On a rack of silk

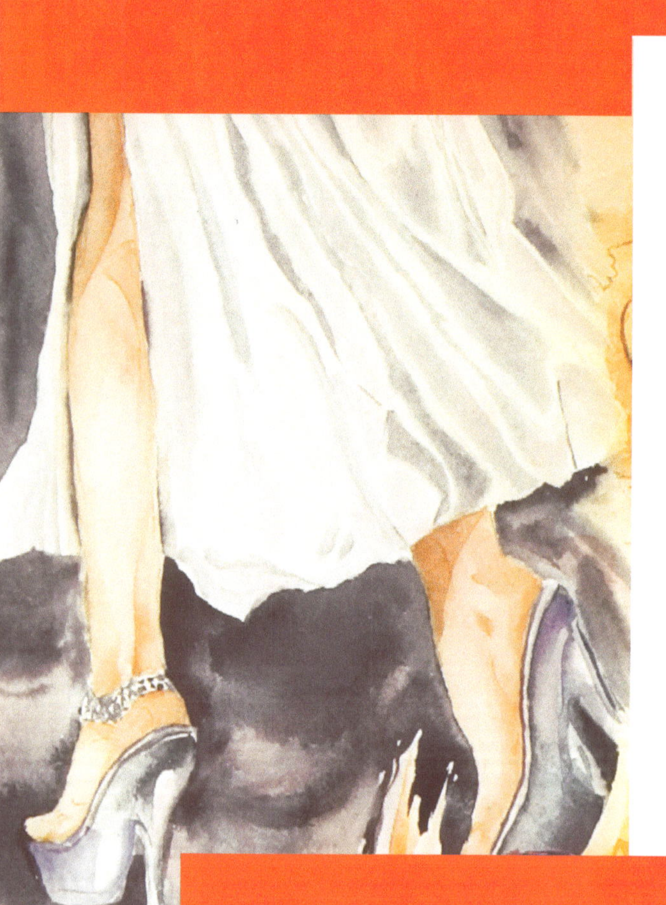

Dressing for the Occasion

I wear long billowing dresses
    lacy garter belt
    snug silk stockings beneath
Nothing else

When a dancing spring breeze
    swirls its teasing path
    up under my skirts
I feel your sweet hungry mouth

The Garden

I approach your hole.
The darkness attracts me.
Oh to be inside of there!

What is this scent I cannot smell?
All your holes are mine.

Yes! She says, dripping juice sublime.
My face is there as droplets fall, watering the garden,
waiting patiently for new sunshine.

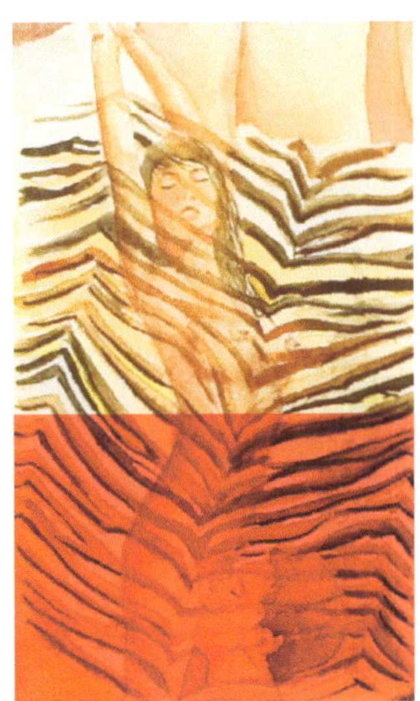

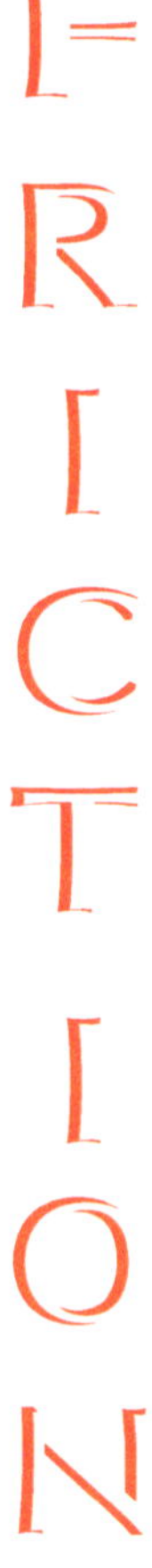

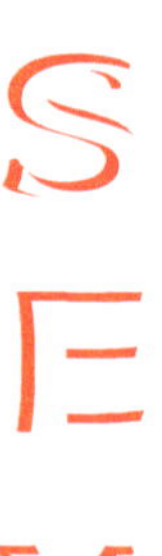

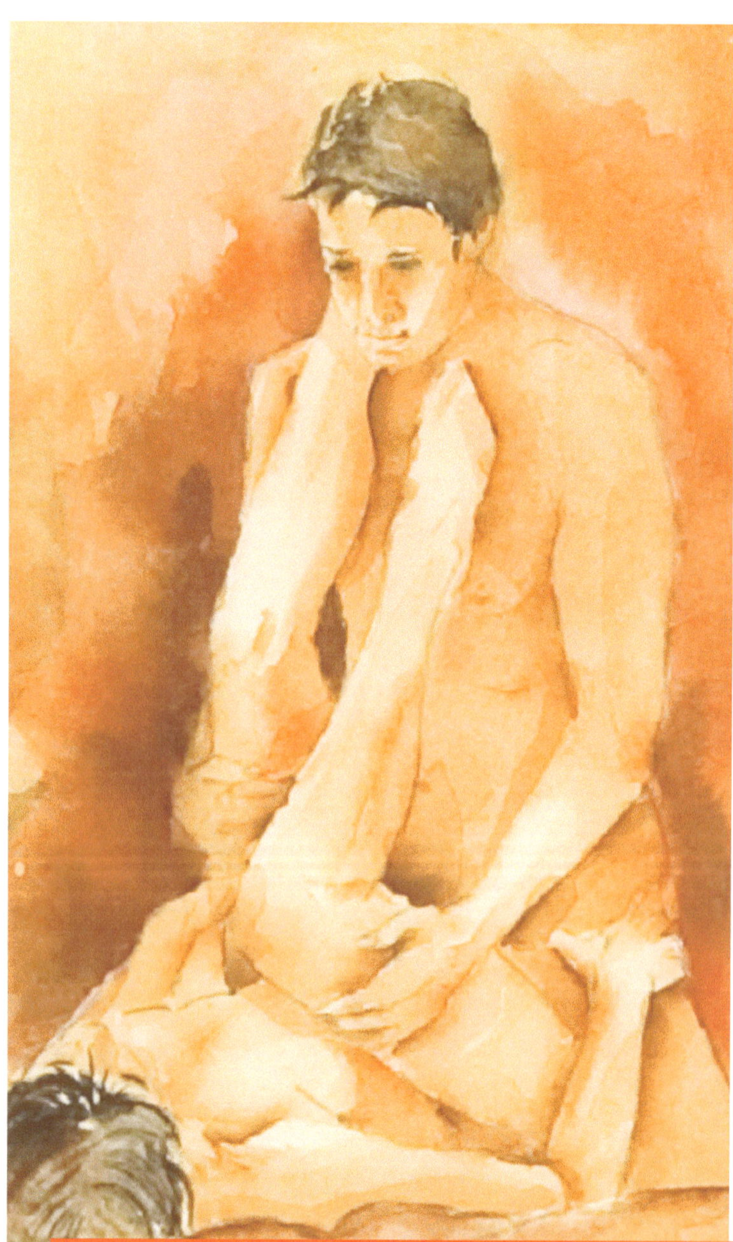

Snake Charmer

Delicately
separating my moist petals
your jade snake
slips through
and in

He turns his head
this way
and that
side to side
relentless in his search
a divining rod
sniffing the well-spring

On the finding he is ruthless
nudging
bumping
he pushes me to the edge of
the garden
and beyond

Coping

Whenever he takes himself from her
the leaving rips a great jagged wound
which cleaves her from breastbone to anus

Her heart
        dangles out twixt the raw flaps
                naked
                        bloodless
                pulsing with misery and desolation

In earlier times
she had attempted to set it back in place

It would not stay
        indeed would thrust itself out
                with even greater violence

Now she simply allows it to hang
        slender filament of connection stretched
                almost to breaking
                with the heavy wait of days

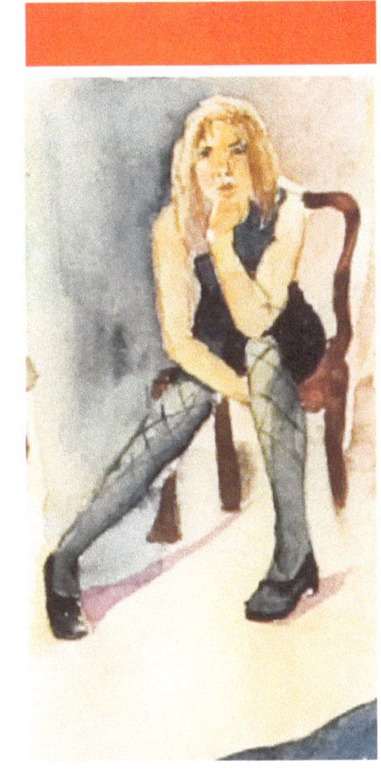

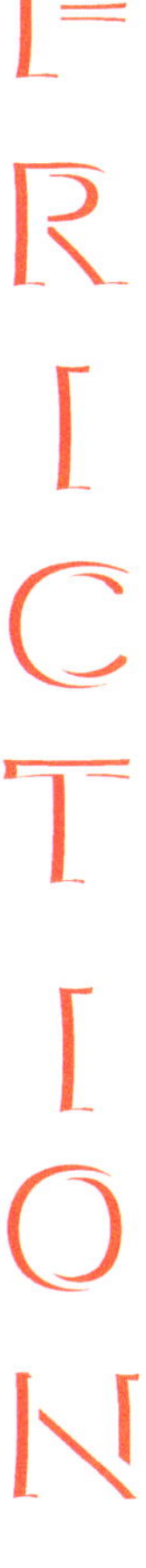

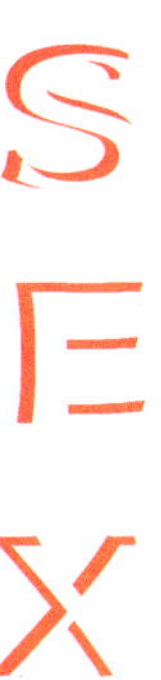

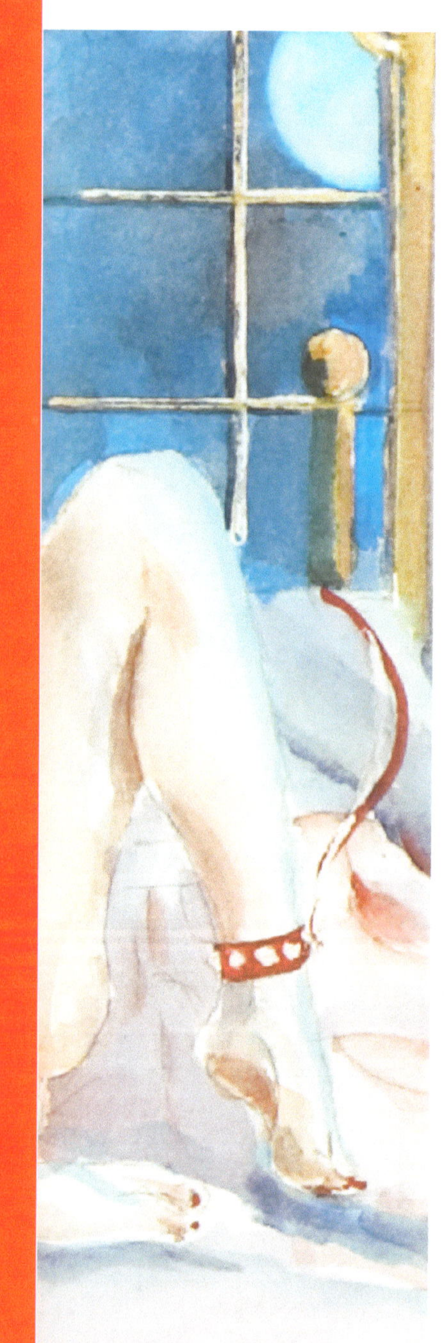

Preparations For a Business Trip

Before leaving
I kiss your torrid lips
then attempt to lull my hot
pussy-on-the-prowl

I tie her firmly
to the foot of our bed
where she strains against the leash
of studded red leather
spitting and meowing
in feline rut
until I return
to release her
for your tomcat touch

Because I Was Born in 1950?

When I was growing up
young women did not speak the word
COCK
they gnashed it
moaning
in their sleep

So the young junior miss
who hungered for the nourishment I
knew would flow from
coupling
dared not sup
but only fantasized about...

Dark young hoodlums
met in theatre balconies

Pulsing
steaming
pool guards headed for their showers

Brazen road labourers
with promising eyes
provocative hands

In time day dreams became night realities
gobbling forays for tidbits
that did not quell my appetite
but whetted it to distracted craving
I fed voraciously yet starved

Until somewhere
gradually
along the way
I sloughed off the ragged snake skin
of fear and taboo

Hunger was still my mate
although not clawing and biting

it simply was
and I accepted it

It left me vulnerable and free

Free to dine
at your banquet table
to unreservedly feast on the
abundance you offer

Free to stop
rest
satisfied
nourished

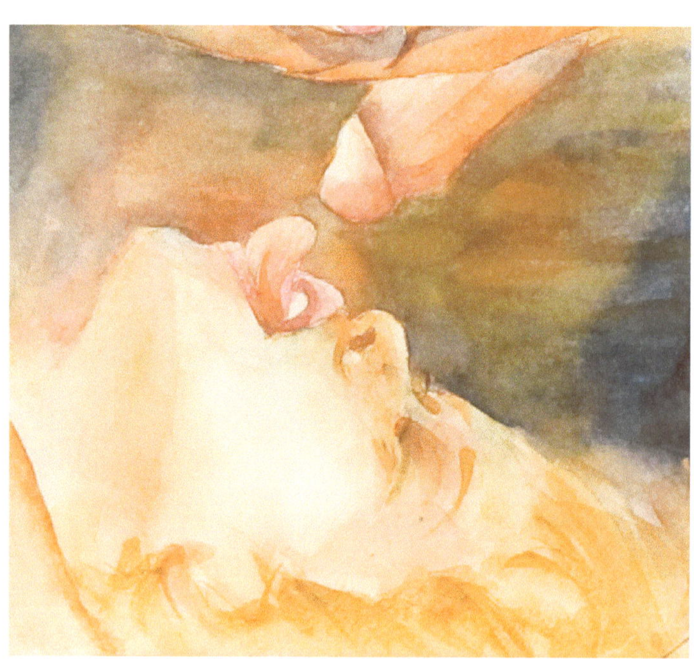

Dinner

My mouth waits
          open
                    hot
primed to devour you
          in snarling nibbles
                    licks
          of lust
from forbidden gate
          to stalk of jade
in places hard
          and soft
scented with primal musk

COME BE MY FEAST

Sweet Meat

Take the hardness of me
by surprise
it erupts from sleep
deep night outside

Sucking mouths make
many mongrel noises
mixing
whipping
whooping
it upppp

Shaking and scraping
flesh
heats
red
blushing
blotches
of
blood
bonding
sex
Cooing sounds pierce
my fierce
armour
of mask made
out of fruit

So, defenseless
and breathless
I
make
you
wait

Until I think
you are ready for
the piquant pungent
plump plowing prick

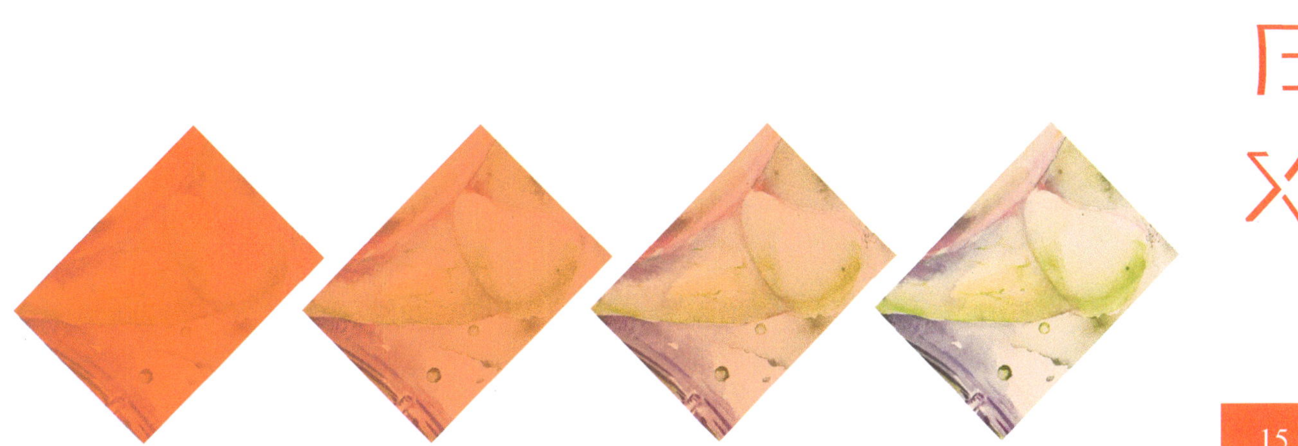

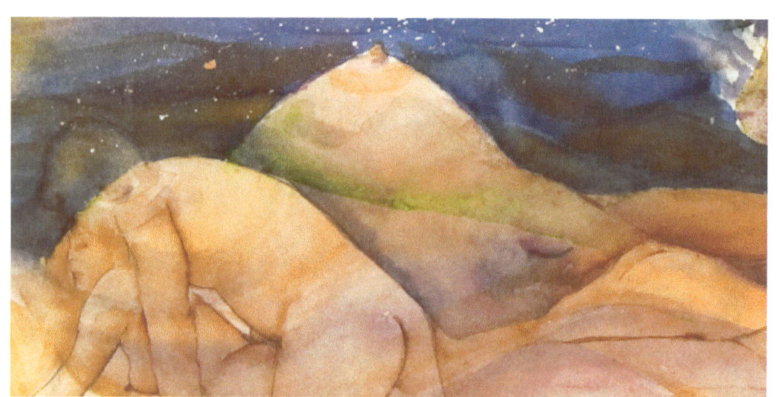

Plunder

When you are
        ripe
I will plunder
the territory
between soft mountains
and the valley's
        green vegetables

Luong Phat

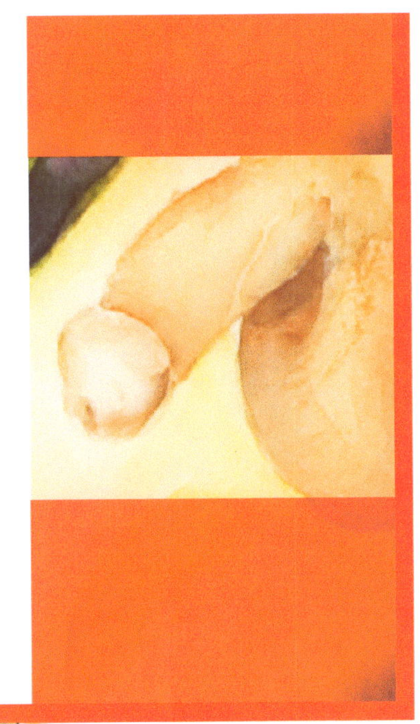

What is smooth and shiny
wrinkled and tiny
short and tall
big or small
hard and soft
lifts you aloft
Rams into the breach
backs out with a screech
Has no fear of heights
looks great in tights
It pumps and it squirts
oh how it flirts
It spins and turns
some say it burns
Erect posture it has
and responds well to jazz
Rock and rolls in delight
try some tonight
Is generous and brave
or may act like a knave
It dances and wiggles
to the sound of your giggles
A musical organ, a mystical joint,
you get the point
Ready for lickin'
with the name of a chicken
All red, white and blue
saying "I love you"
COCK

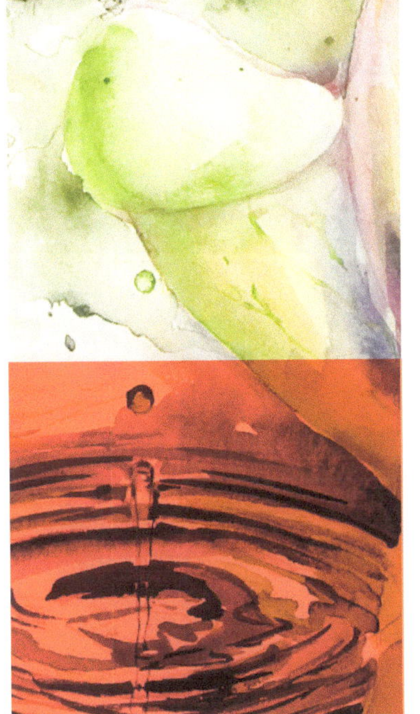

F R I C T I O N S E X

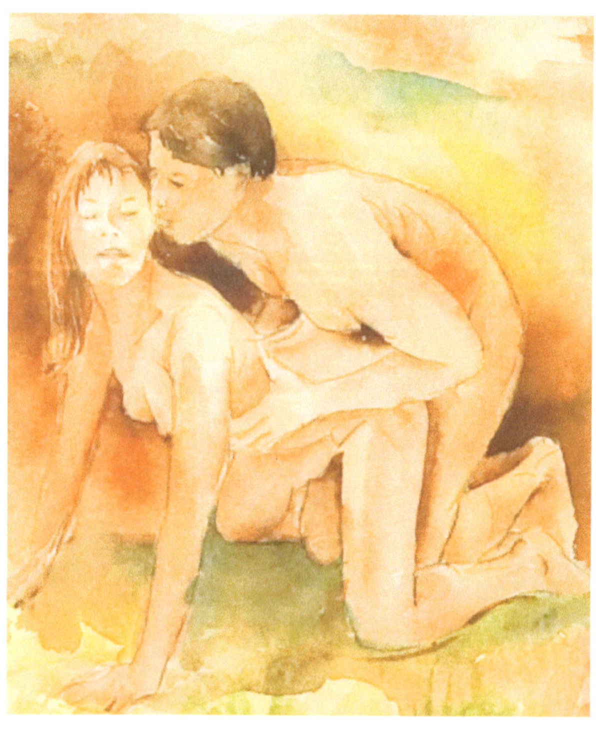

My Stallion

It is a hard thing he carries
this bone in his pocket

Sometimes the weight of it is more than
he can bear
It pulls him down
and around
and in
without discernment or conscience

In pursuit always of only the one/but all
the musky well-spring
the place of life and death

Where it can sniff
and prod
and ram
and spew

He feels Madness in its quest
Madness
and Glory

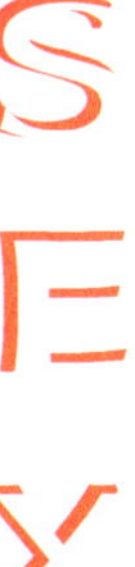

The Way of Your Choosing

My lover beast
When next your fragrant plums are ripe to bursting
so weighted with sweet nectar
that a single piercing stare
might slice their velvet skin
with loving attentions I wish to make of you
a Sacred Fountain

You must then, tell me
"O blessed woman
now is the time to let fly my essence
and this is the way of my choosing

...kneel before me
with rounded mouth and slickened tongue
lave my staff and my jewels
ream my dark cup with gentle fingers

...oil thy luscious breasts
slither slide them round and down
my piston rod
smooth as jaguar's engine

..lie across the table
v-legged
pulse thy fragrant garden to me
push it
very hard
very fast
along my stalk of jade

....stand spread-eagled
titillating thy honey pot
whilst I oogle
and playing hard upon my flute
blast its crescendo full upon thee

...head to my feet
tongue to my toes
slither thy pussy
slow and tight
up
down
along
my shining pole

...present thy marble peach
wide-split
that I may climb upon thy back
and ride the wild jungle beast

Yes O Blessed Woman
now is thy time for the sacred fountain
and this is the way of my choosing"

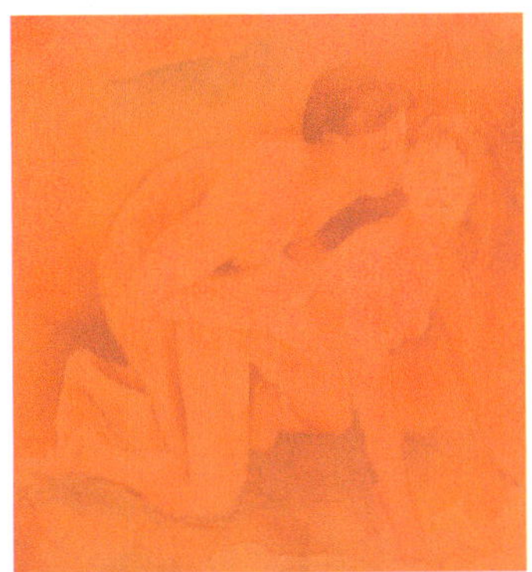

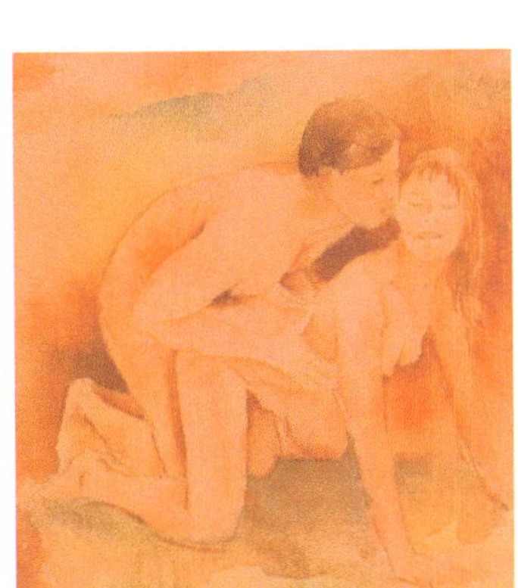

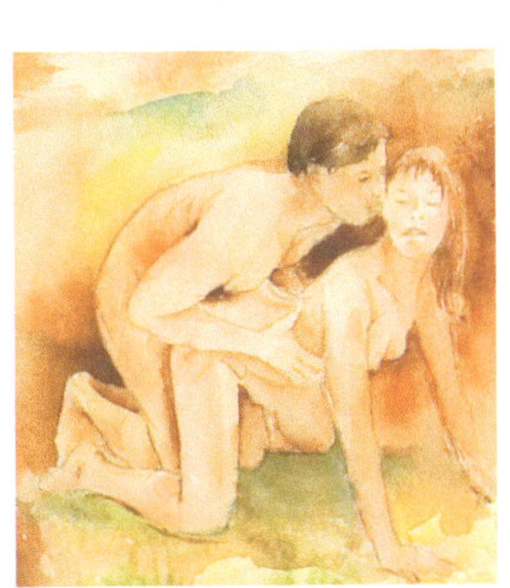

We're All Animals

Mating muskscent thickens the air
        croons
"Come sniff me
        wild wolf of the striped pelt"

Warily
        swart, moist muzzle
        pushes into my pungent bush
        whiffs hot
                jumps back
        alarmed by the smell of humanity

Cannily
        knobbed tongue
        slicks out
        whelps pulsing vulva

Odour/taste pictures scorch fevered feral brain
        midnight rut
        hot blood
        woman flesh

Yellow glazed eyes
        rock
        in hard skull
he laps rabidly
        saliva
        love juice
                drip
                from sooty fur

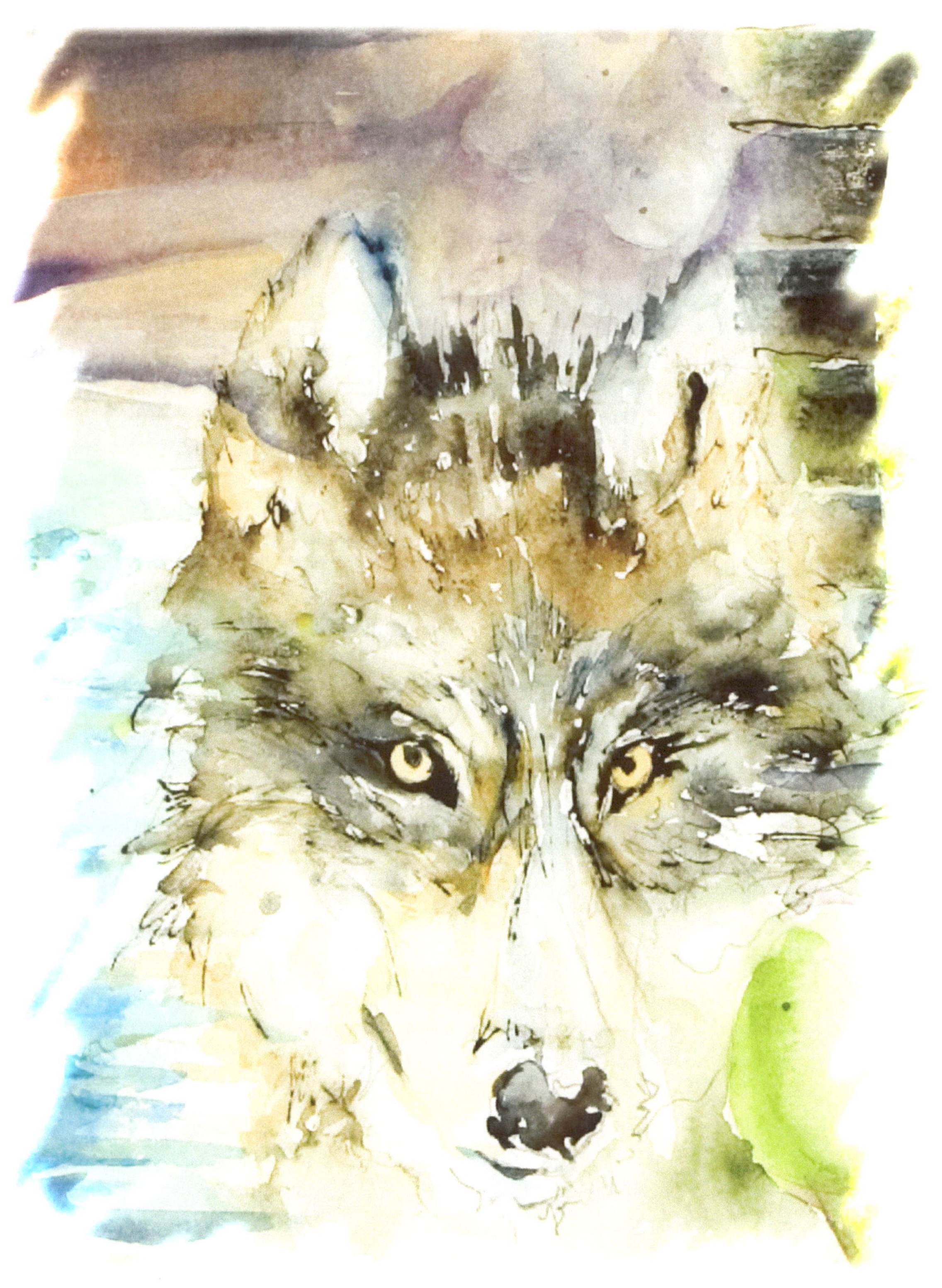

FRICTION SEX

The Battle

The lines of battle are drawn. As they square off, she strikes the first blow, just before he cracks her open. By now she is dripping blood. Their chests heave mighty gasps, seeking oxygen to feed their desire. He crushes her below his weight. She screams.

Her eyes are animal eyes. Her bites are tracks across his back. His slaps are tracks across her bottom. With super-human effort she is able to throw him aside and she manages to secure him to the chair with leather straps. The leather smell mingles with his musk and she startles them both, squirting cum into his face. It is her cum and she retrieves it with hungry licks. He squirms as she tortures him, sticking things in his holes just as he did to her. This makes them equal. Weapons of love are arranged upon the table. Some glisten, some shine, some are dull and heavy. His eyes bulge with anticipation. There can be no escape, but by some trick of the imagination the roles are reversed. She finds herself bound face down and blindfolded. She is entered from behind. Once again her cries announce the penetration, full and devastating, leaving no room for doubt, nor for anything but this total awesome magnitude of inestimable size. Reality vanishes leaving this wolf, this gorilla with genitalia, this ferocious tiger where only moments ago was a man in the flesh. Finally they are finished, spent, undone, waiting to be put back together again. After all of this they hold each other with divine tenderness and fall into a sweet sleep. They later look back and see their naked bodies at peace.

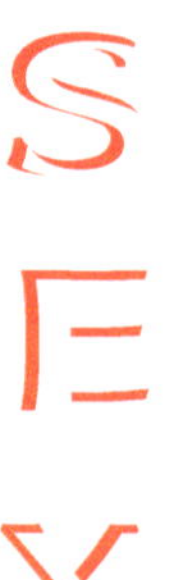

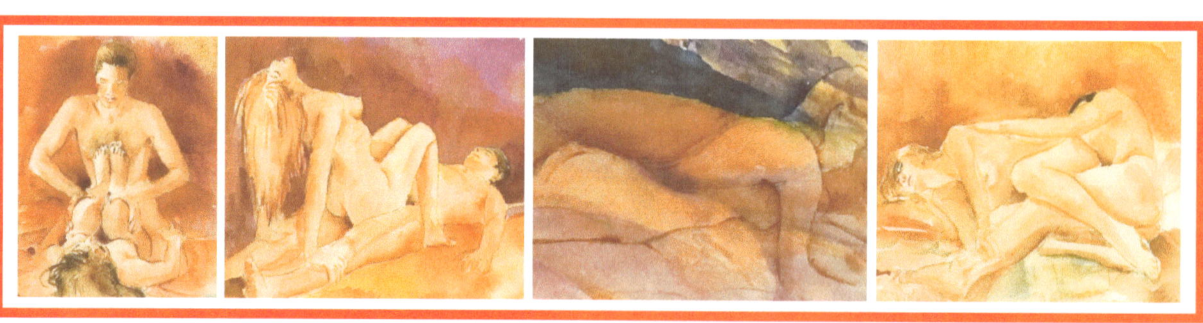

Beast

Sabre-toothed
        always hungry
she lurks in my interior forest
hoping to devour you

When she prowls too close to the pristine edge
        they of the light hearts
        and cherub bottoms
drive her back
        with laughter
        flung from pouty mouths
Their honey love soothes her
        She believes she has eaten

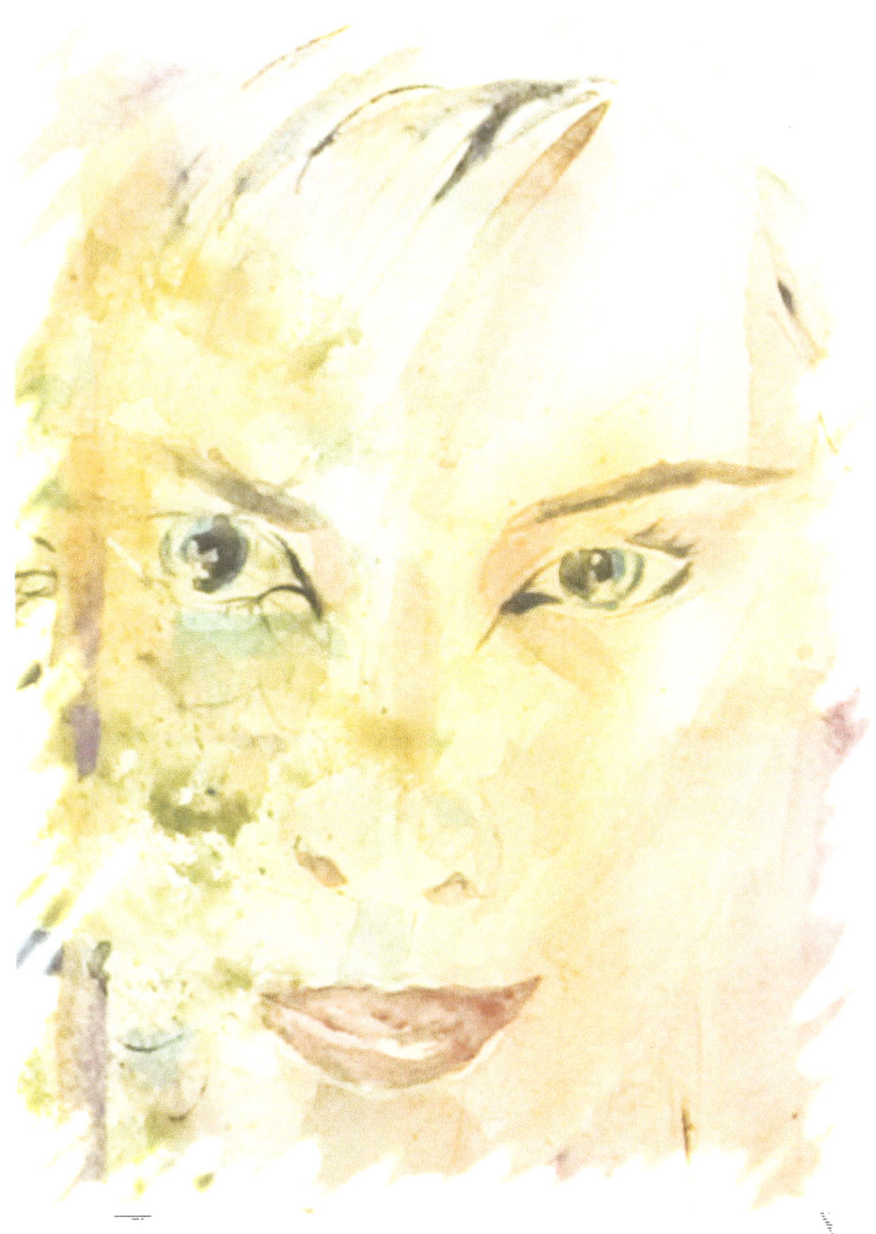

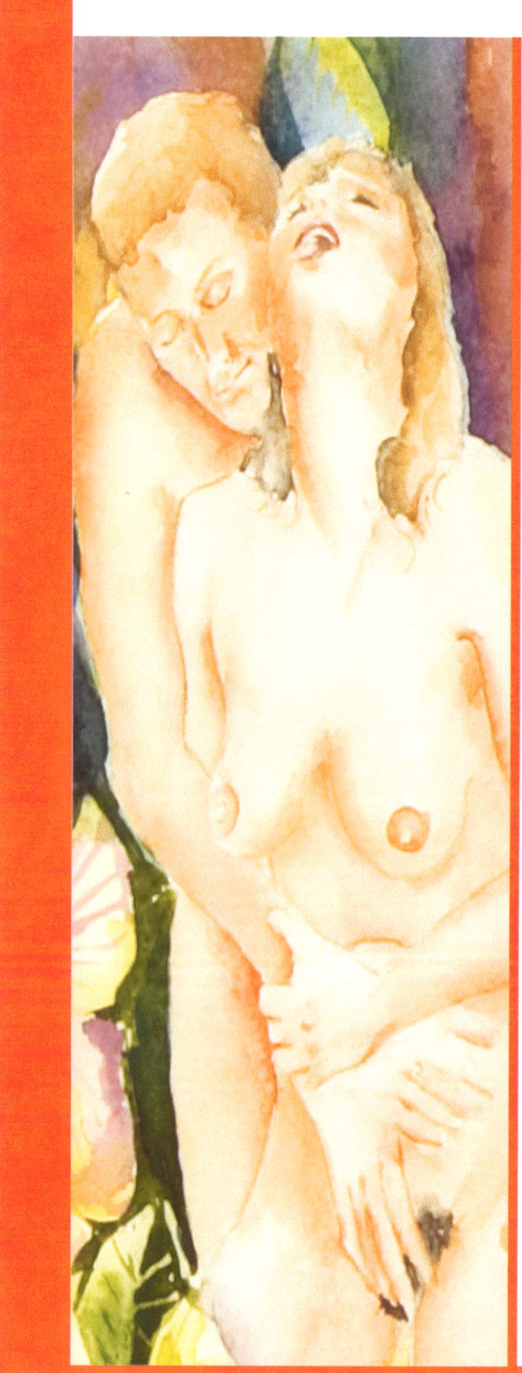

Here We Go Again

You come to me and the Hunger begins
    Blunt teeth
        nuzzling
        gnawing at my innards
    Rasping desire
        so agonizing
        so exquisite

It skitters up
    through my body
    leaps from my eyes straight into yours

down and round it roils
    twists
        surges upward
pulling our ragged breath in tow

Lusty breakers wash over me as
    unseen
    you press your palms against my nipples
My skin sighs
    it's only the beginning

Horn of Plenty

Blow the horn of plenty
the fountain of life
into glass delicate
lips of flower blossoms

pushing
        pulsing
                pleading

for the most sublime
attention
from admirers

near
        and
                far

as the south pole
and northern hemisphere

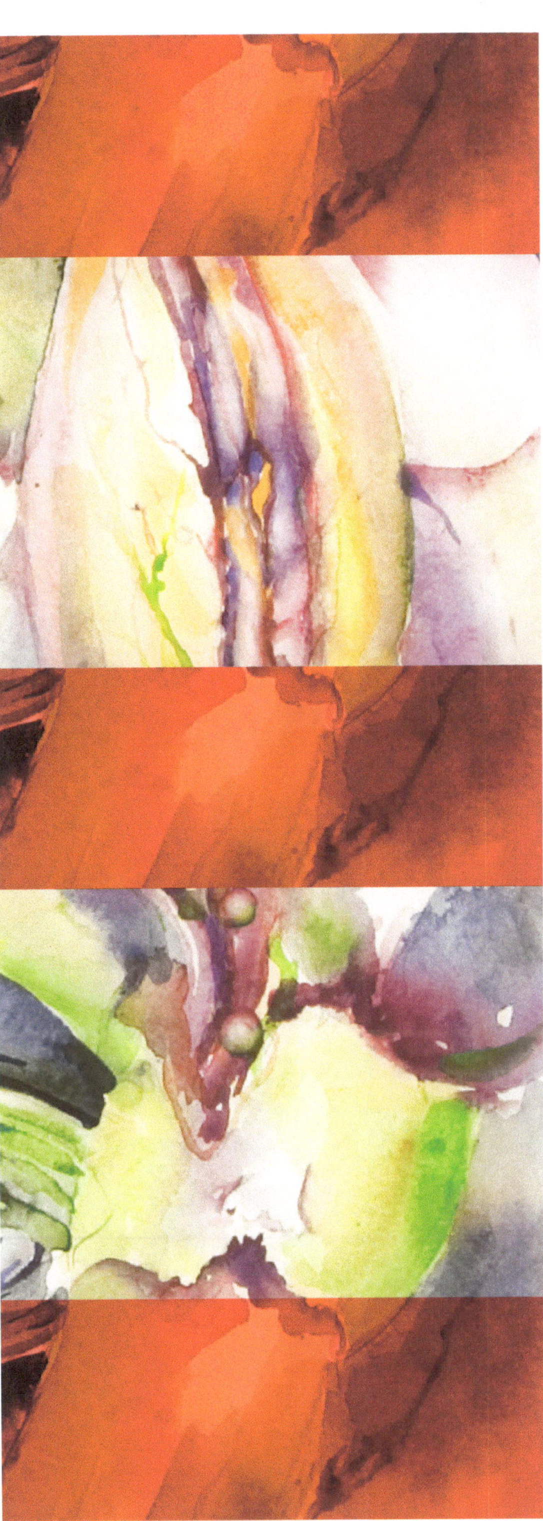

Yes I Want You To

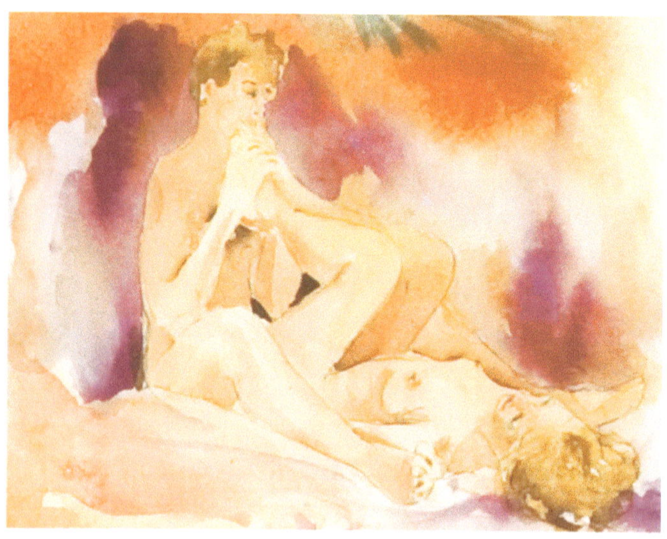

Undress me with your eyes
Bore through silken layers
    to velvet screaming skin
    where nipples
        teeth-eager
    protrude
    and succulent primed meat
        dances

Strip away flesh
    bone
To elemental flame
    the core of white heat

See me
Know me

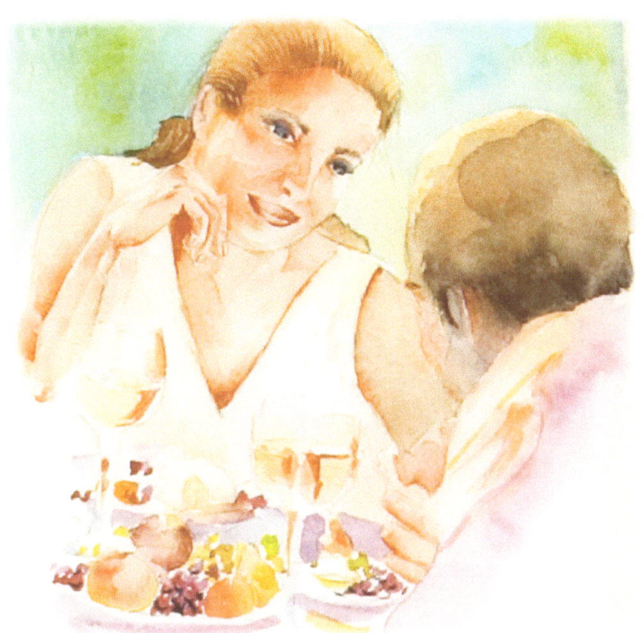

Touching

My love reaches across the table
with eyes like fingers
that feel me all up and down.
I shiver with anticipation
of other touches with other parts.
Our words meet and mingle
like hummingbirds competing
for space at the scarlet feeder.
Then we settle into each other
and feed the need for
stimulation, comfort, and succor.
Longing, desire, and lust melt
from our psyches and drip
sparkling life and renewal
in these suits we call our bodies.

ENERGY SEX

Energy sex goes far beyond the physical. Hearts open fully in vulnerable surrender to each other. Deep emotional connection paves the way to sexual ecstasy, wherein lovers become their lovemaking. Energy bodies and auras merge in a union of sexual bliss.

Coaxing Colour From Love

Beneath your pulsing lid of skin molten
lava rolls

Icy green neon
streams through to my finger probes
ruthless mouths that roam
sucking along your arched limbs

laughter and screams
merge in your quaking
collapse

Massaged spots leak green
Sparkles on to the bed sheets

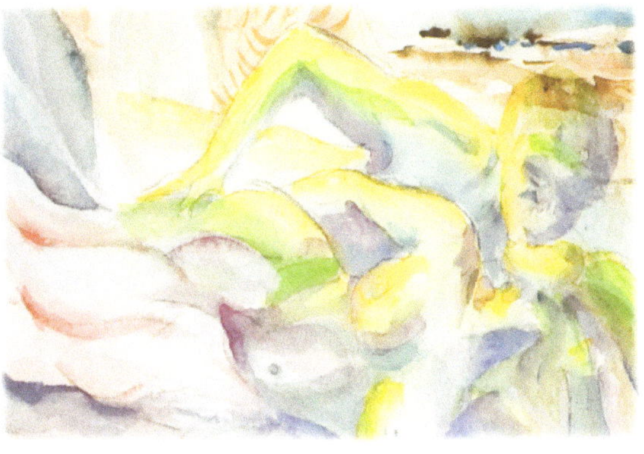

E N E R G Y S E X

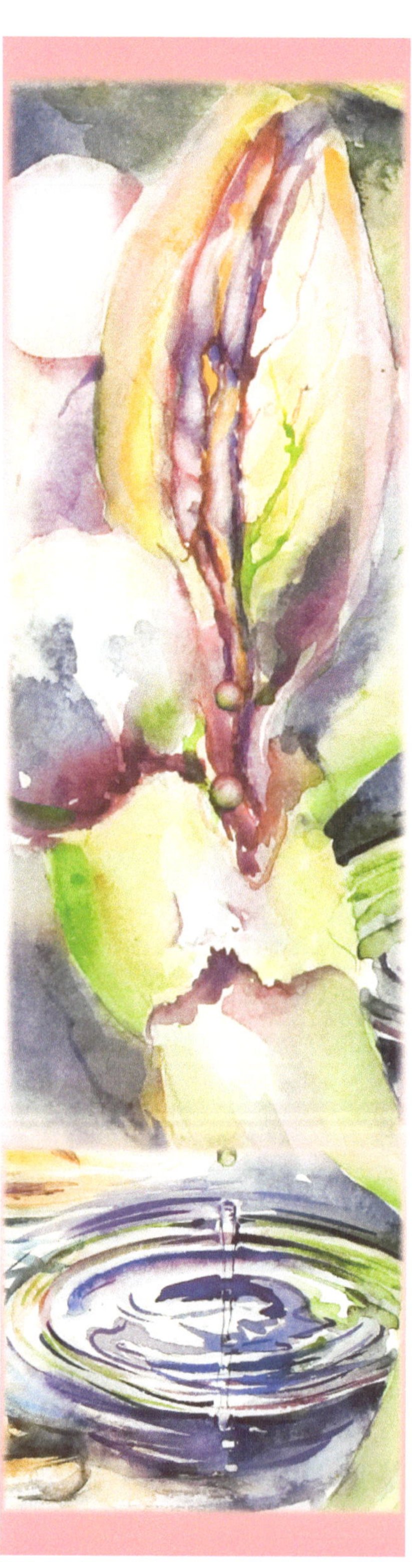

Sucking Senses

My sex charges through
to yellow, then green,
purple and white.

My ears can hear
the vibrations of those colours.

They pound up my coiled snake,
then float down to my belly.

Sensuality drips from
your curves
feeding nectar
to my sucking senses.

Aftermath

You rewarded my fragile trust
with a caring, deliberate tantalization
    to beyond self
Orchestrating my abandon you left me transformed
    outwardly satiated
limp and spent
But inside! Aquiver with love's powers

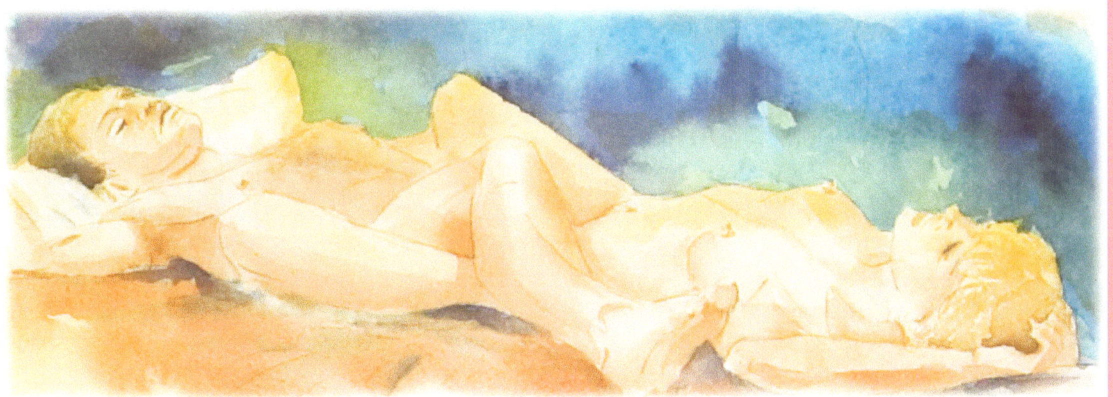

E
N
E
R
G
Y

S
E
X

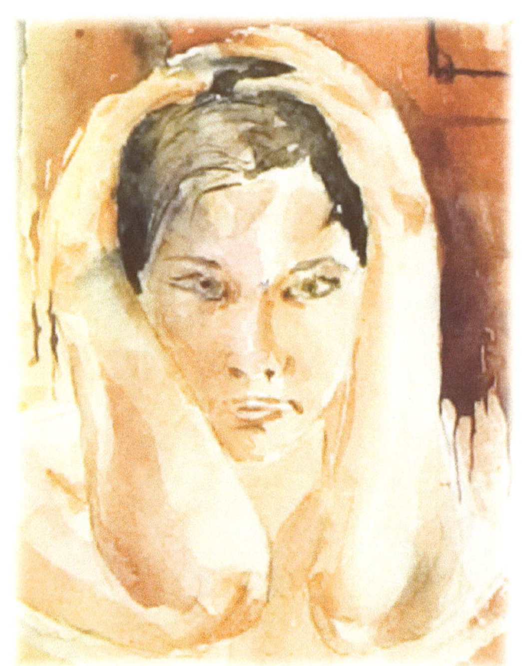

Seeing

The lights went out
Only then could
We see without
Our eyes.

Sometimes We Get It All Backwards

Withering fires burn in scornful eyes
where compassion's tender light should shine

Cold knives whip out from tongues so sharp
that could instead give sweet nurturing breath

Iron fists rain bone-crushing blows
when a gentle caress would do as well
or better
to bring us close

Are we so afraid of love that we must
hide in its dark shadow?

We want so much to reach out
but too often our open hearts take a detour
through our closed minds
and then
We just get it all backwards

Bad Love

The same afflictions affect both kings and peasants.
Not only syphilis, but love also.
There is a bitter cruelty which loved ones inflict upon each other.
It is surpassed perhaps only during war time between enemies fighting to the death.

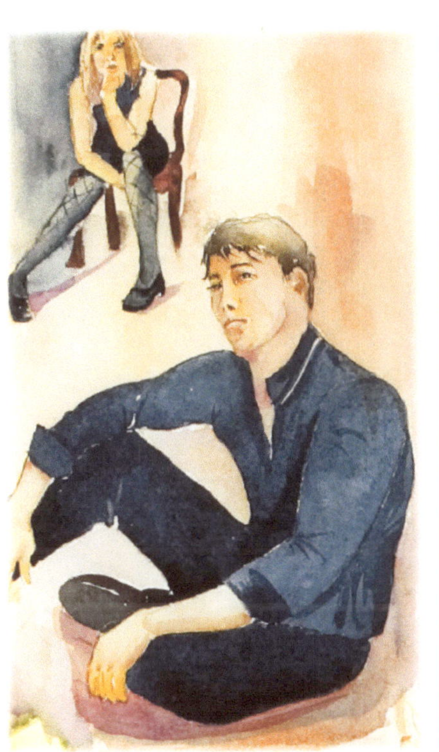

Tin Can

My heart does ache
but there is a little stingy padlock attached
it is flimsy
and my heart bursts open
at certain moments
How the lock gets put back secure
I don't know
You can't pry your heart open
unless you want it to resemble a tin can
If all else fails, try love.

ENERGY SEX

The Perils of PMS

Hate crept in today
through a tiny bloodstained crack in
our love

How dare you hold a mirror up to me
and smiling
say
"Look in there
see the coward"

I looked at you instead
and wanted to smash
your head
with the great black frypan
that owns our kitchen

Union

One and only makes two.
These two are one.

Yes Indeed He is Her True Valentine

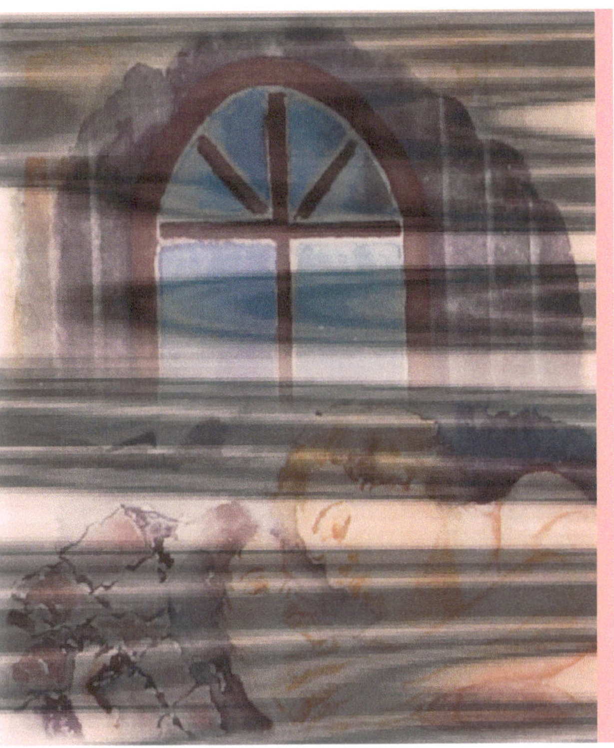

In the depths of night
she can no longer discern their separate
heart beats

Each pulse
is the throb of One

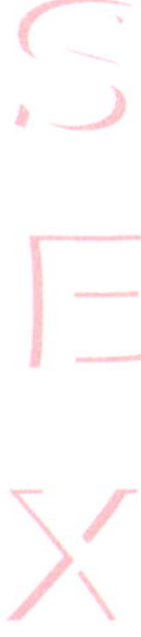

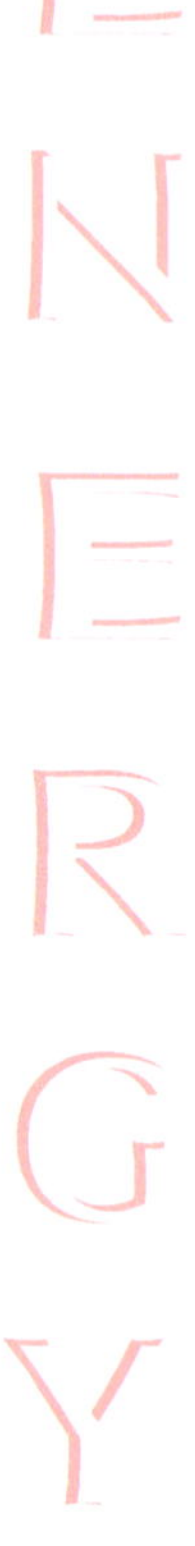

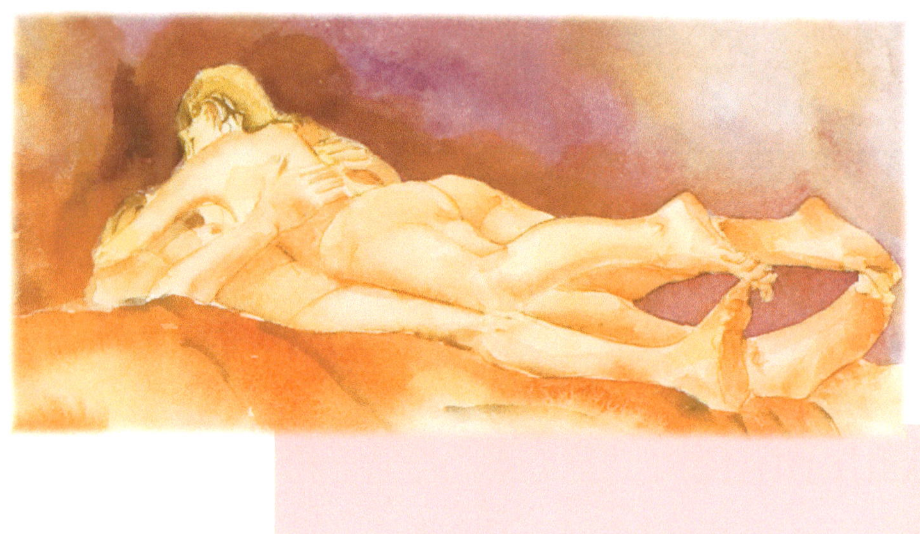

Pianissimo

When a heart opens
completely
to love
The song of its surrender
tickles the lips
of dreaming virgins

If I Could Paint Like Chagall

I am a sleeping valley
    deep and lush
    shrouded in mist

When my lover comes
    I awake
shooting stars into the night

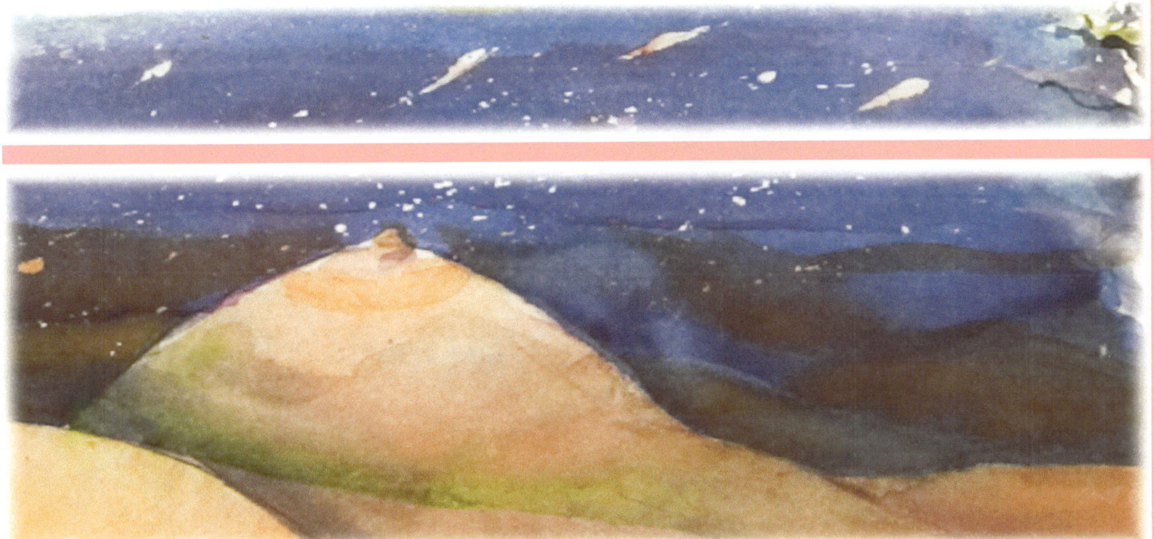

E
N
E
R
G
Y

S
E
X

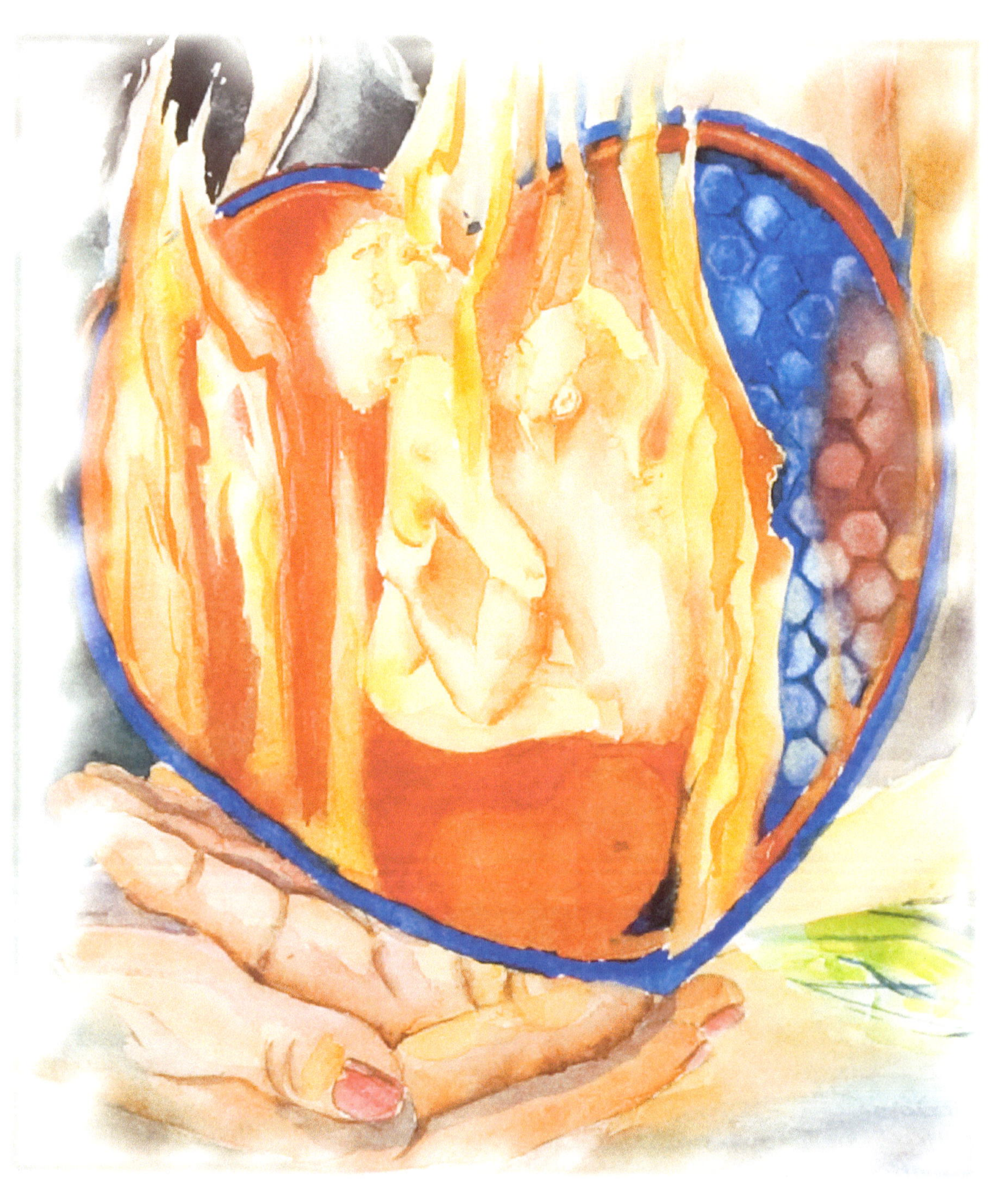

The Gift

My heart belongs to you

It does not come to you through capture
by teasing it out on to my sleeve
and stealing it away

Nor by pinning it down
a vampire stake
through its hot centre

Oh no!
I have given my heart to you

I trust
you will hold it gently

Giggle

There is a giggle in the middle of my heart.

ENERGY SEX

Wrap Me Up

Entwine me with your body
Wrap me in comfort
        and ecstasy
All sinuous curves
        and sharp angles
        with one long
                hard
                plumb line
        straight up to my heart
Zzap!

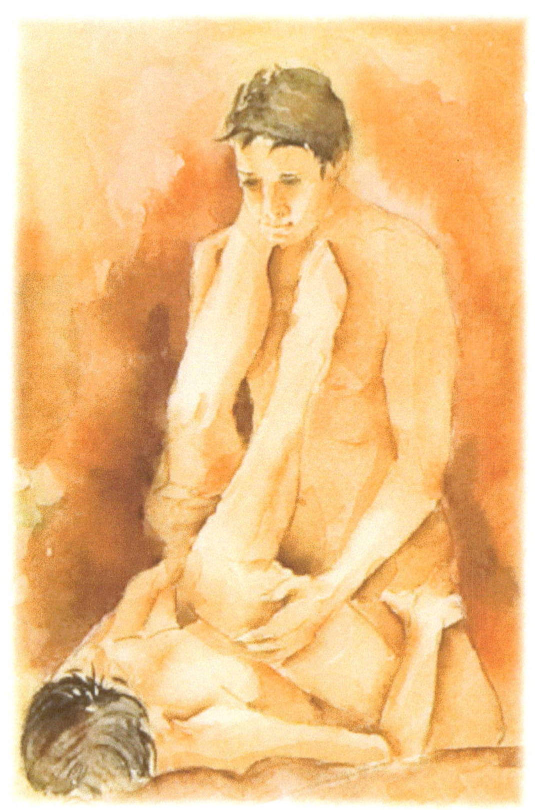

What's Next?

Surrender to me my beloved
    and wait
    turgid-pricked
    for what may come

Ferocious vampiric hunger?
    piercing throat
    humping buttocks

Tender carnal adoration?
    dew soft ball licks
    dainty cunt squeezings

Astounding subtle/raw delights
    close in
    ecstasy is imminent

Fear has no place here
    where all is love

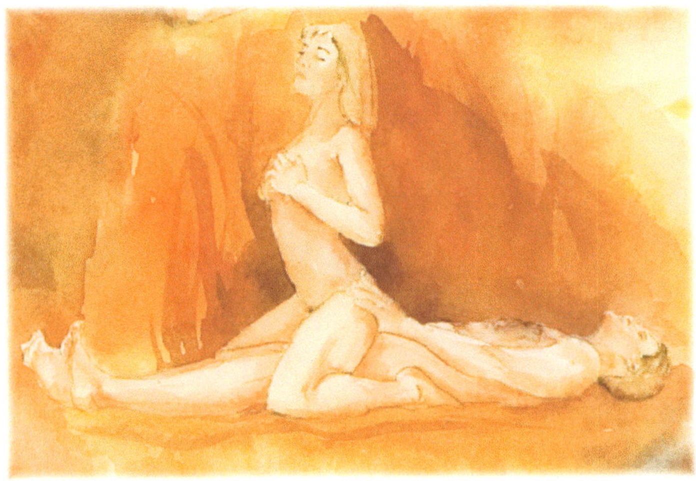

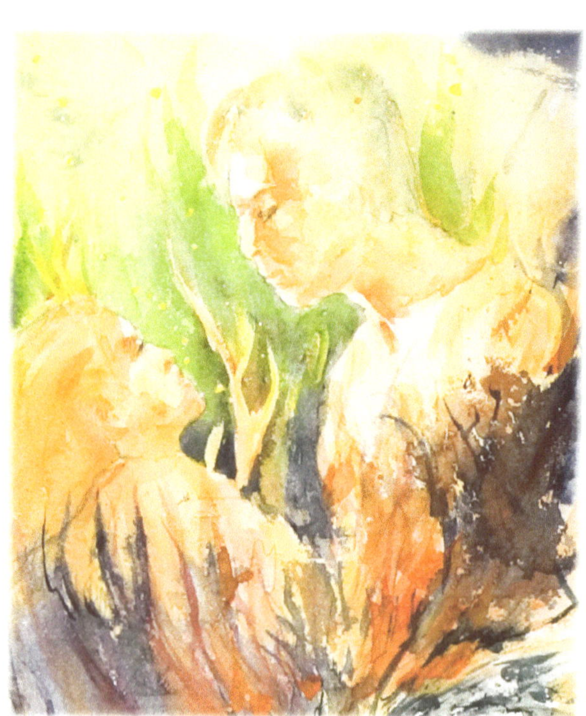

Moving Through Life

The blackness of the pit
swallows them

They can fight against it
be chewed up
spit out
sucked-dry souls
bereft of light

Or

They can surrender
in the darkness flow
Emerge whole
shining brighter
from the rough polishing of their
passage

Beauty

Heart opens
    on a razor's edge
hanging from a slender golden
    thread.
When hearts are open beauty is revealed.
When hearts are joined beauty is created.
Is there any way you will stay forever?

Choosing Love

Love is not much like Pepsi
or marbles
It is more like air
but not really
Or ideas
yes like imagination and fear
limits and numbers and boundaries
don't apply here
but intention does
focus does
choice does matter

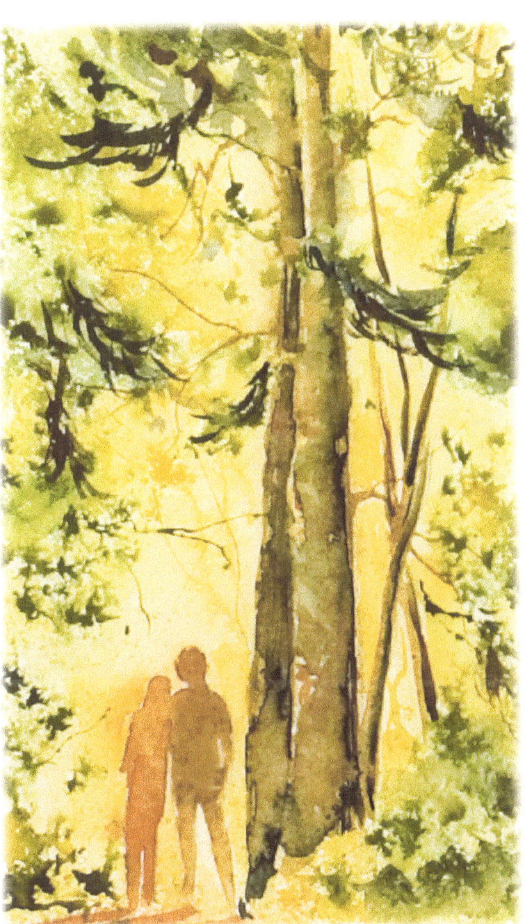

Evolution

You are changing

The man I first met
isn't always there anymore
a new guy's peeking out

He's a little more shy
a lot more vulnerable
He listens to others
doesn't always need to prove
HE knows the right way
In fact
He's not at all sure
about the right way
or even if there is one

Surprisingly
that doesn't make him afraid
but fills him with wonder
and anticipation

He's at home in his body
likes to touch with it
share its warmth
with others

He's a fierce fucker
riding me with a bang-on perfection
of bone welding
skin melting
blood churning
LUST

That's not to say he's all thrust
no stroke
Ah no
he carries tenderness too
and calm

Sometimes he carries me
when my New Woman stumbles
on her way out
She's readying herself
for the man
you're growing up to be

Building Our Home

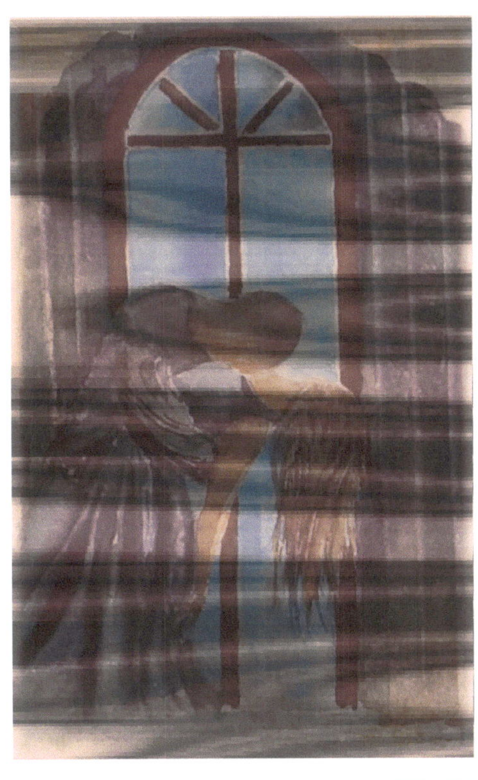

In the dark of night
    the witchwoman and her priest make their
    magic
no powders or potions do they employ
no incantations
Flesh and spirit alone are their instruments

And so they begin
    Her body crushes to his
        undulating this way
        and that
    rythmically inviting entry

    His turgid wand knows the way
        rams deep

In pleasure/pain
    she bares her teeth
    hisses
    moans
    presses in for more

Their writhing pulls energy from the earth
    from the trees
    from the very air
    and the watching stars

Each thrust intensifies the power
    coursing into her
She churns and swirls it
    squeezes and guides it
    with a shudder
        and scream
    shoots it out into the floorboards

In bonded silence the shaman pair move
    place to place
    over the construction site
    performing their ritual dance
        for walls
        rafters
        window frames

Each outpouring an augur
    of fulfillment
    fruitfulness
    the Whole
    numinous consecration of their future

House Consecration Day

Hey you, O you, you MAN
Come take my hand
NOW at the start of our journey
Take it and don't let go, EVER

O, there will be times when you can hold it loose and easy
When all is flowing smooth and silky

But a firm grasp will be needed too
When I fly too far ahead down the paths of adventure
Or lag stubbornly behind

And when the fears come
Then you must hold on most tightly
Only to relax and cradle
Lick my palm, suck my fingers, bask in the warmth of my hand in yours

Yes MAN take my hand
I'll take yours
Perhaps then we can reach
the end of the journey together

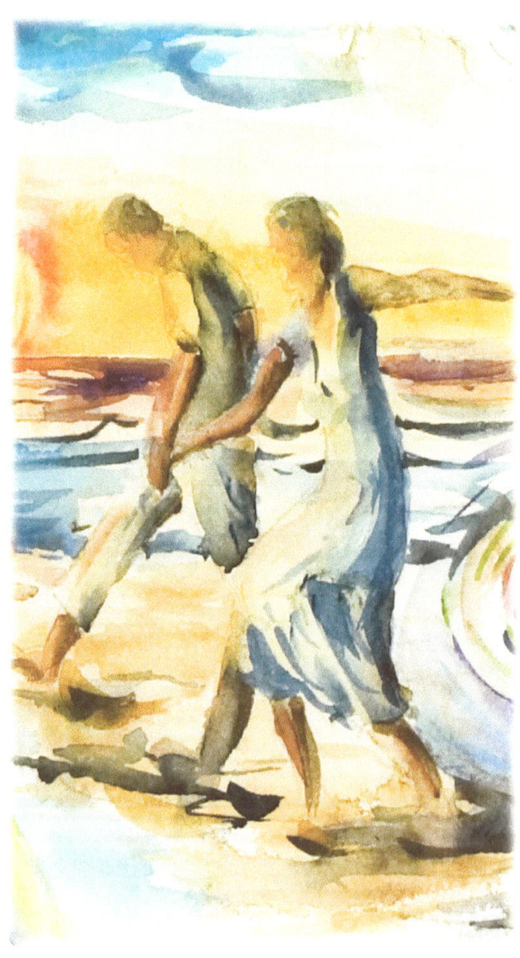

Come Lie With Me

When world weights crush down
        come lie with me my love

Sharp-pointed bone edges
        give way
        to soft pillow curves
                in my hammock

We'll rock
        cradled in love
        through sturm und drang

When our swaying stops
you'll be so light
you might just float away

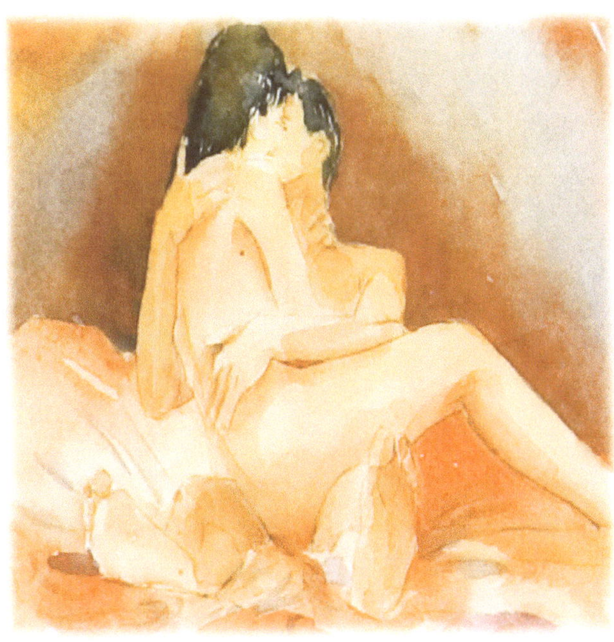

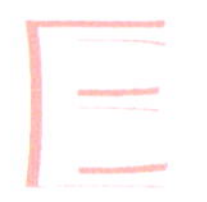

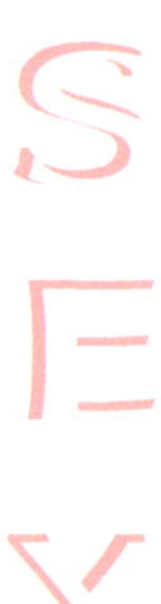

Floating

I had the strangest experience Leo.

I am a balloon.

There is nothing resisting my floating off.

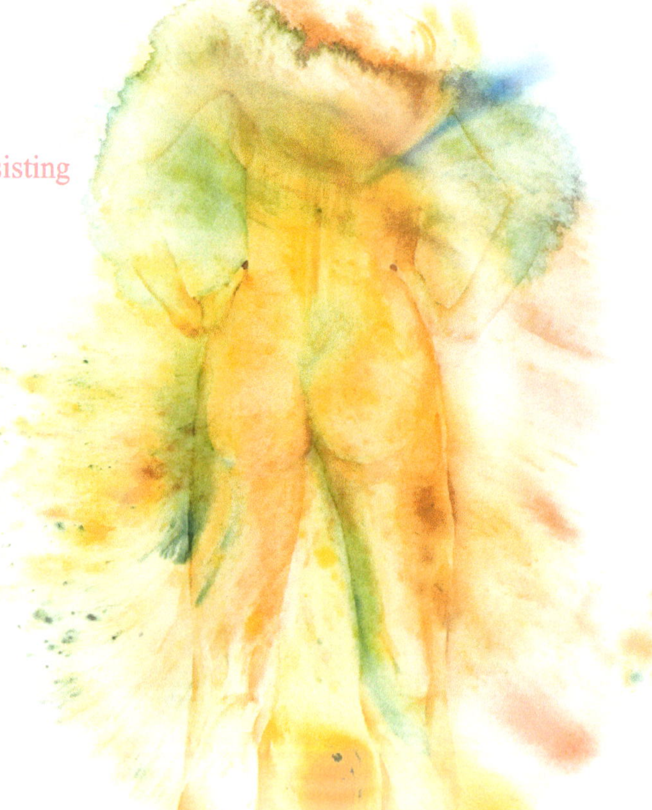

There is nothing pushing me away.

I am free.

SOUL SEX

Soul sex lets go of all control. Lovers are utterly transparent, open to one another and to the Divine. Emotionally naked, physically satiated, reverent and joyous, they unite mystically with the All - the most profound love imaginable.

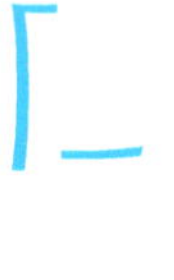

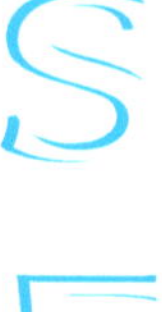

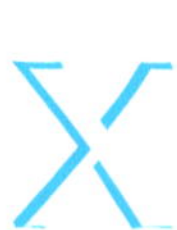

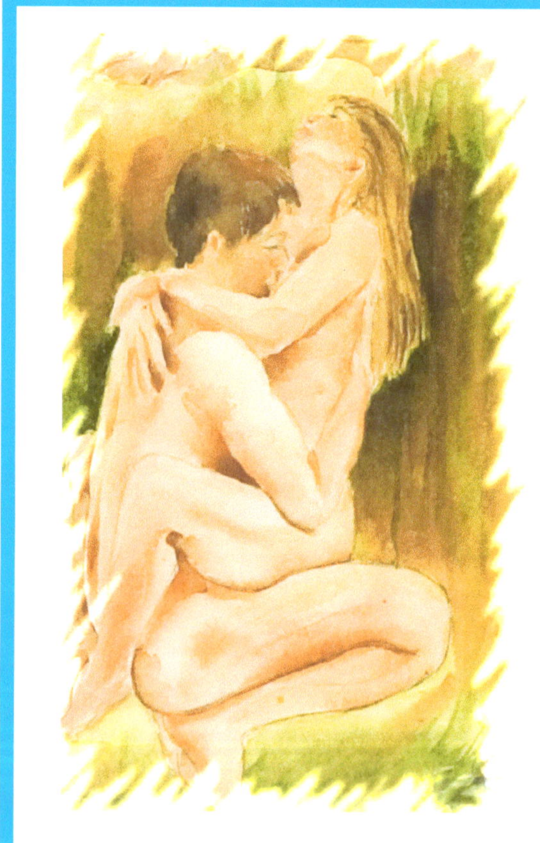

Joining

Through silk-soft skin
　　our hearts meet
Pound hot blood
　　across paper walls
　　to cosmic union

Surrender

Hearts made sweet by surrender
to each other
Souls made sweet by surrender
to God.

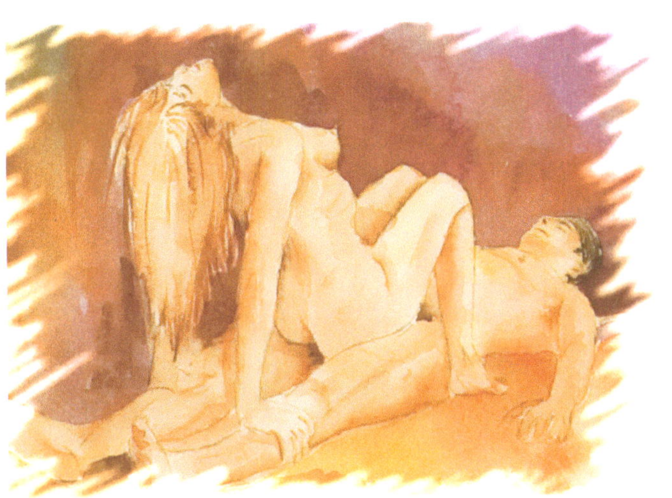

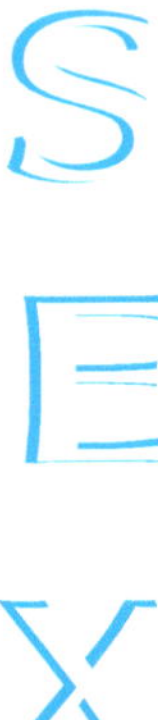

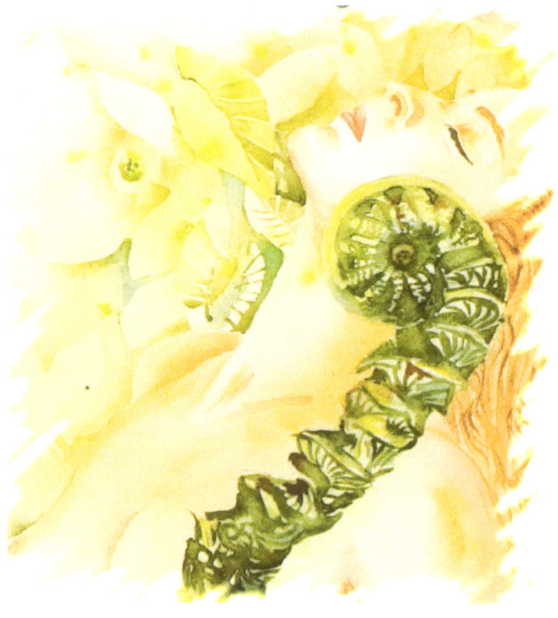

Feeling Fertile

Curl up hard
inside me
I want to feel you unfold
in the warmth of my sun

A fiddlehead flowering to fern
a ripe nut popping

Precious seeds riding my winds
float high and high
The heat does not consume them
it nourishes
transforms orphaned acorns
to mystical oaks

Sweet Mystery

Sweet mystery,
carnival of light.
Around the next corner,
over the next hill,
on the other side,
over, under, behind.
I thought I knew,
but I forget
what I thought I knew
Oh yes, now I remember.
Sweet mystery!

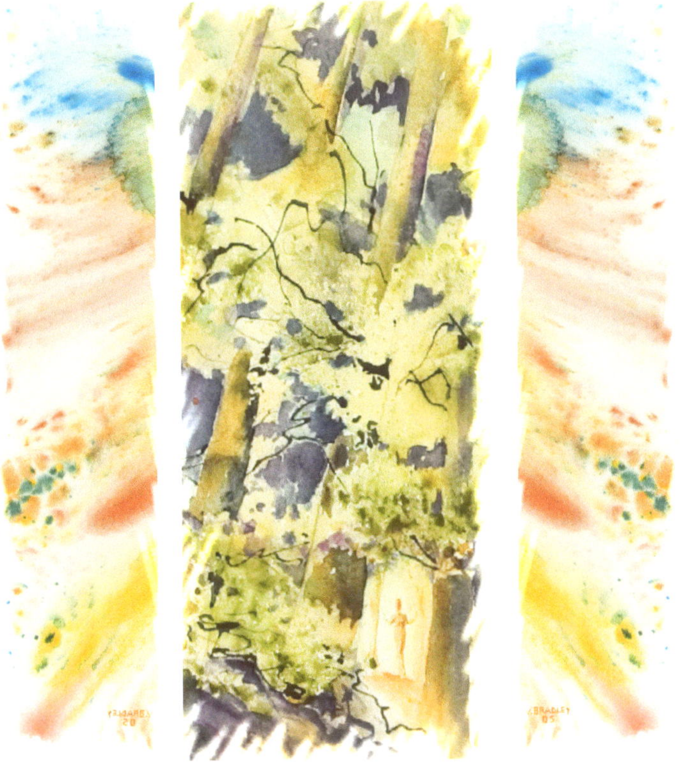

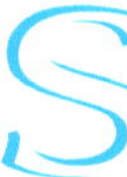

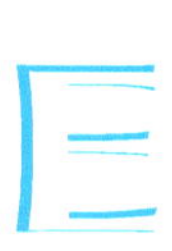

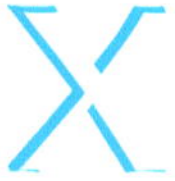

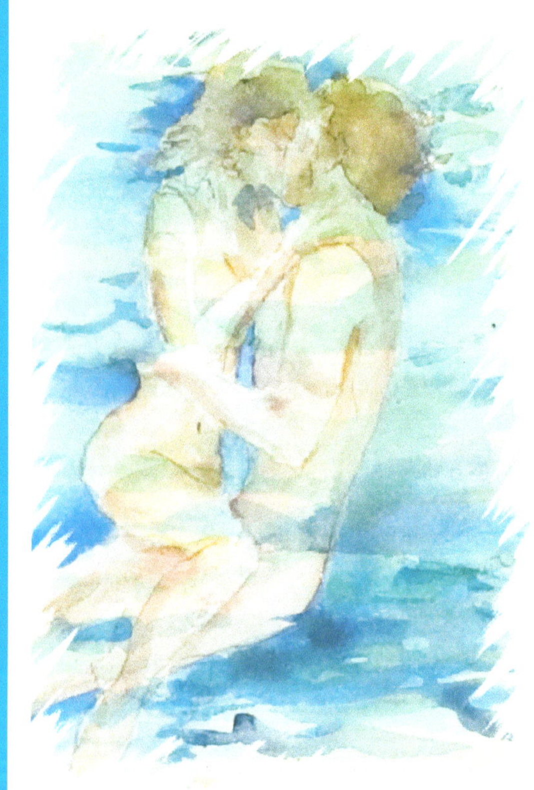

I See the Truth

From the deep well of your soul
bright love cascades
bathing me
in dazzling streams of
ecstasy
Clear dark eyes
reflect the truth
of soft words
moaned
from softer lips

We shall float
Forever
in rapture's warm sea

Vulnerable

I lie here now
naked, utterly vulnerable, trembling
without magical powers of any kind
to summon and control
the forces of material reality.
Mercy, forgiveness, and innocence
are my garments
and my chariot
across the desert between
here and there
where death and self and God are

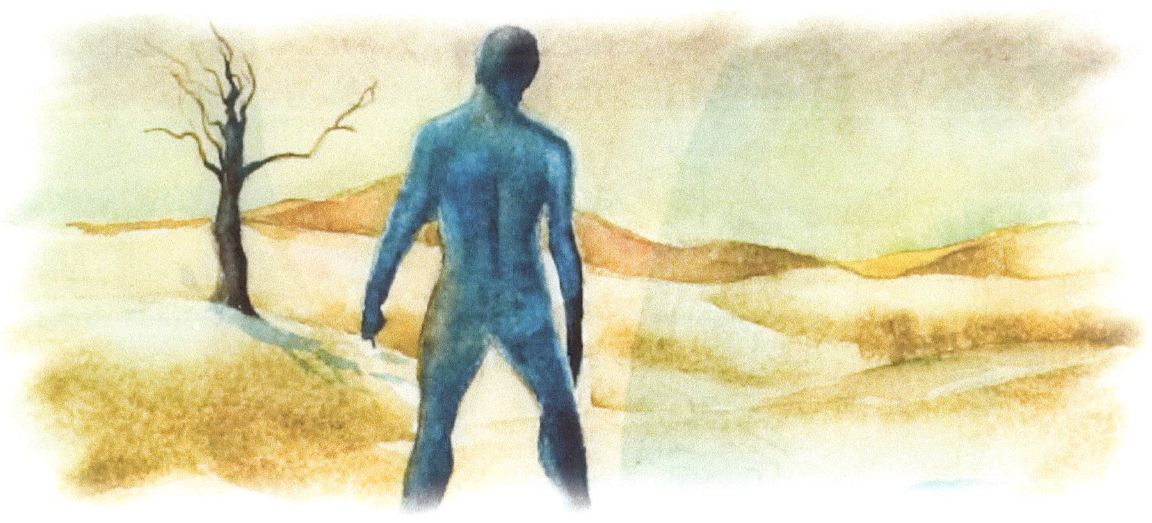

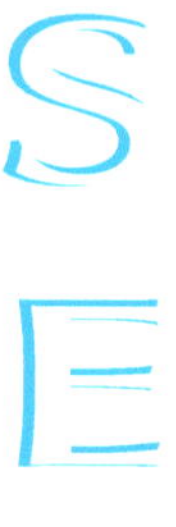

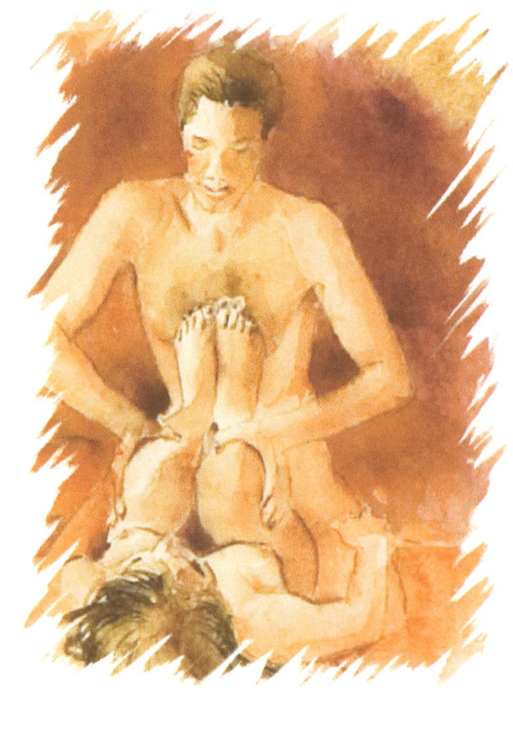

Dance of the Gods

Dance for me my love
Dance for the Gods in you
        Let their light pour through your eyes
                and cock
        Power revealed
                and sanctified

O creator/destroyer
        I offer myself to your terrible beauty
My soul lays bared
        Waiting
for whatever touch you may deign to give

Easter Hymn

On this day of Resurrection
let our holy waters flow
Lash me with your tongues of fire
sacred brands from head
to toe
My body is your lamb to
slaughter
driven on by thrusting
sword
Meet me now in sweet surrender
we are one within the
Lord

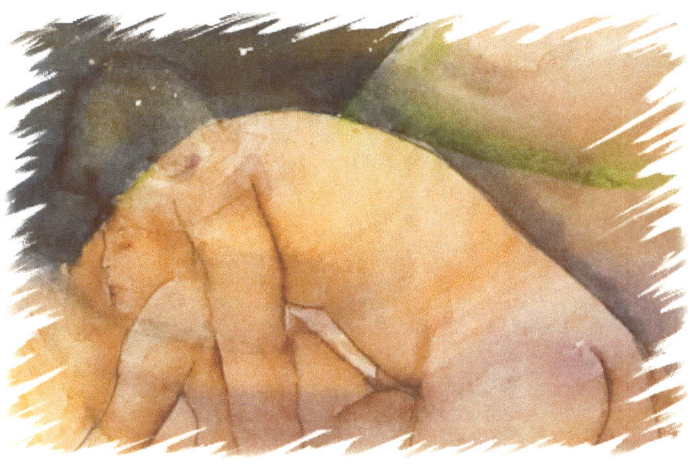

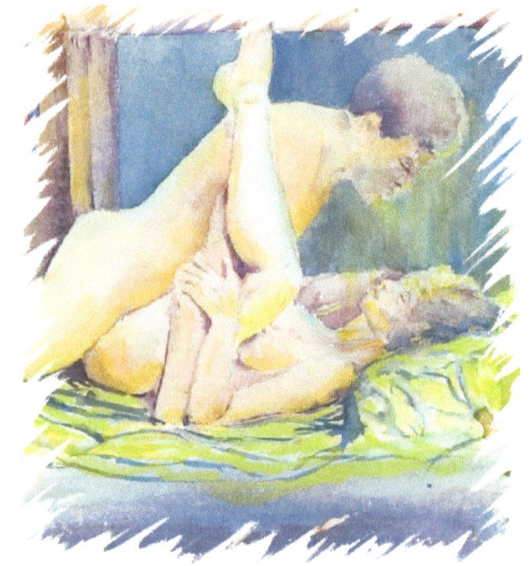

Opening

I am the gateway
You the key

Enter me
open the ancient twisted lock of isolation

Pass beyond to oneness
Our tight-bound circle
solitary flesh
frees the limitless sphere of
all-embracing spirit

In Gran Bahia, Samana
With My Beloved Beast

In heat they came together
in lust's scorch
in the carnal burn for mating

A decade later
on an island of sun and flame
they celebrate their fiery union

A molten coupling
that
combusts their bodies
blazes their hearts
lights their souls

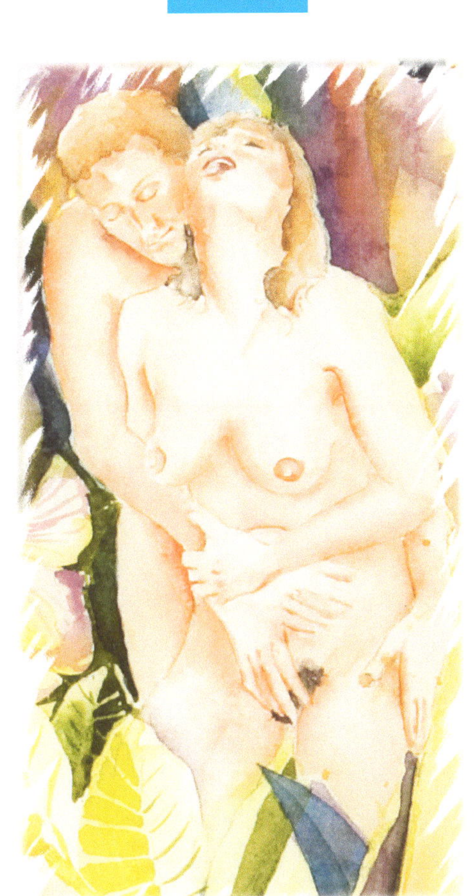

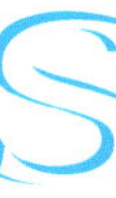
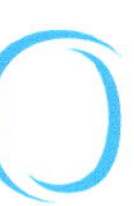
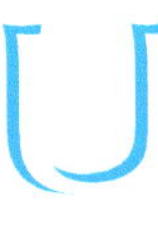

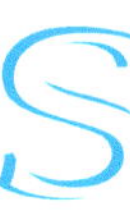
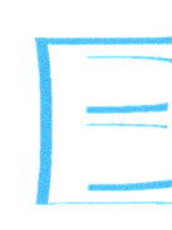
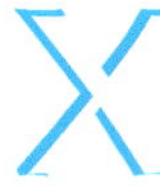

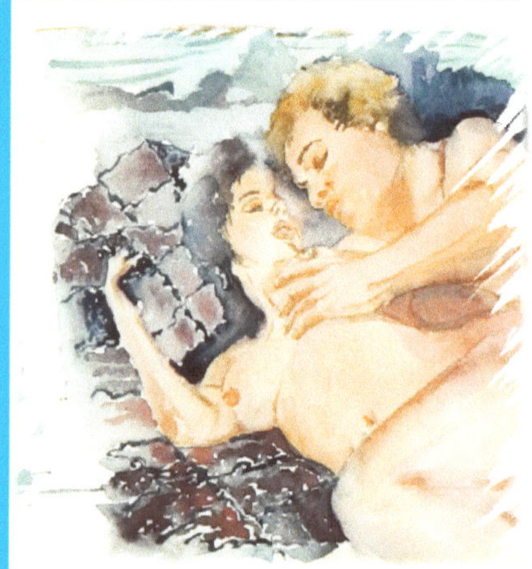

Darling Heart

On this most special day of your birth I give you my love

It is the love of a woman for her man
A hot, wet love that wakes me with a groan in the night and
pushes my hand to squeeze your hardness

It is the love of a sister for her brother as they walk in
partnership through all life's offerings
sharing in delight and dismay with equanimity simply
because they are together

It is the love of one being for another
The spark of divinity that joins us each to each and all to
God

These many loves I give to you
freely, fully, a thousandfold, for always and today –
This most special day of your birth

Vows on the Sacred Mountain

I commit my love, my fidelity, and my time to you, my love, for as long as you will have me. I bow at your feet in honour of your beauty, your divinity and your truth. I eagerly embrace the mystery of our higher selves and our relationship. We and it are unfathomable, beyond words or understanding - available only in experience. Please hold my hand as we journey home to God. When I falter, please lift me up. When you fall behind, I will wait patiently. If it is God's will, may we cross the finish line together, united as one.

I love you. I adore you. I need you. God is my witness as I say these words to you. Until death do us part.

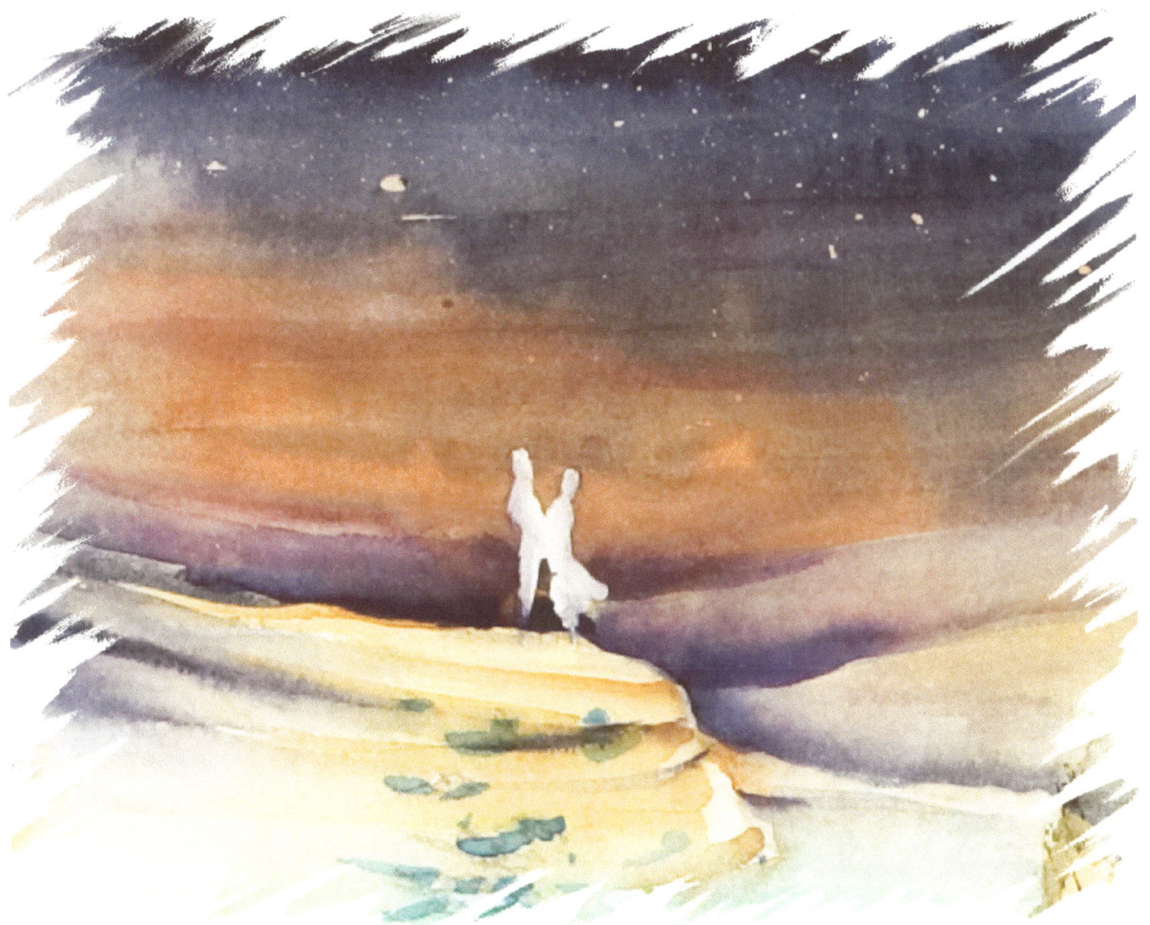

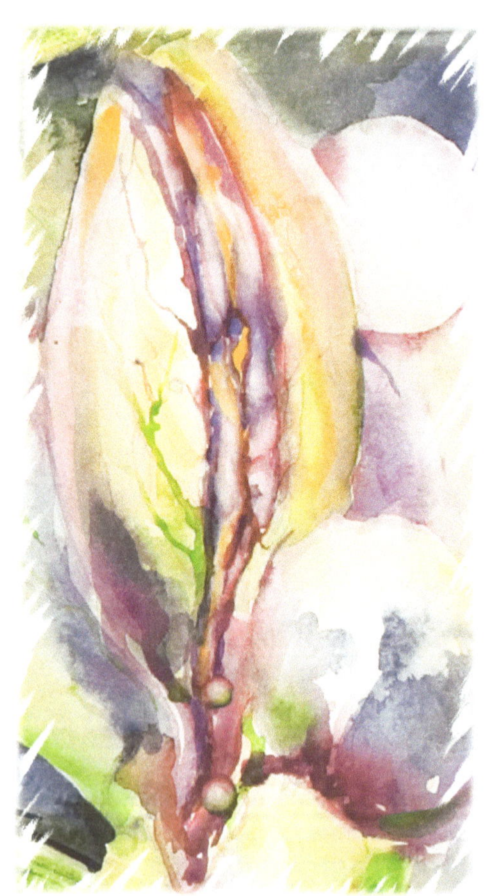

More

Ah, he is the womb-splitter
	He whose skill wrests open her fertile fruit
His power spreads wide her yielding flesh

With love he stretches the ripe chamber
	Until it swells to embrace the vastness of the universe

She flowers within and without
	Child/mother Nurtured/nurturing
	Each and all
He sows her abundance

Seeker

Your fingers are pilgrims
trekking
sacred
across my holy land

In slow reverence they scale the
mountains of my breasts
pause for frenzied jubilation on rouge-
tipped pinnacles

Then trail serenely one-by-one
down to the shallow valley of my navel

A determined dance of piety
o'er the white plains of my belly
A tangled foray through vulva's musky
jungle
Then...

...a tremble, a tremor, a veritable quaking
passes among them
like tongues of all-seeing flame
for "Ah – the Grail is found
sweet mystery of mysteries!"

With tender grace
I allow them entry
to my blessed waters
to my sacred vessel

"Come"
I beckon
"Know the Divine"

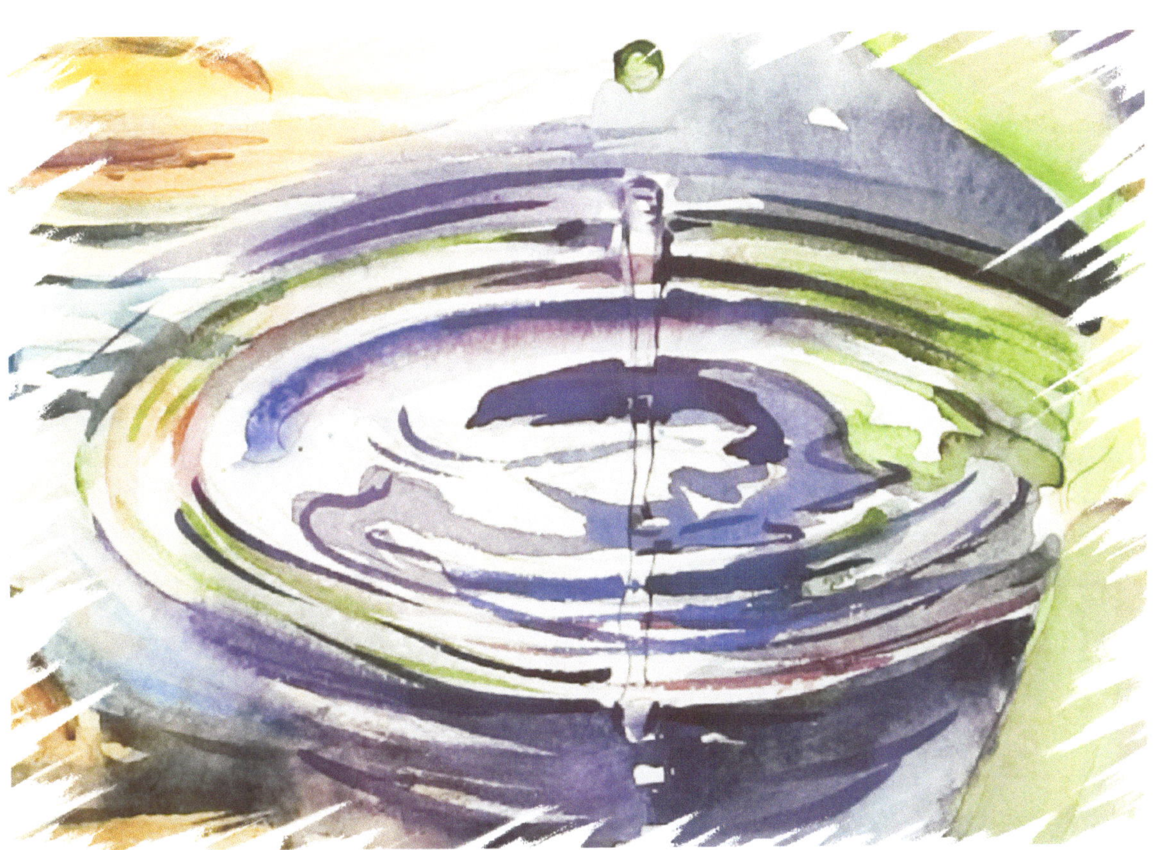

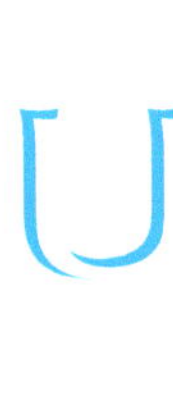

SOUL SEX

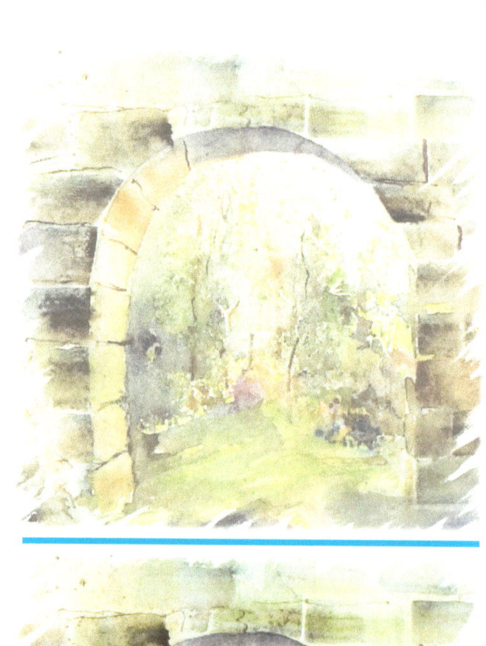

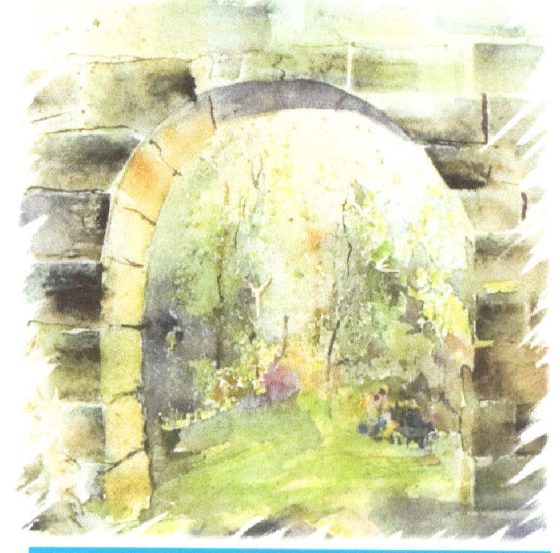

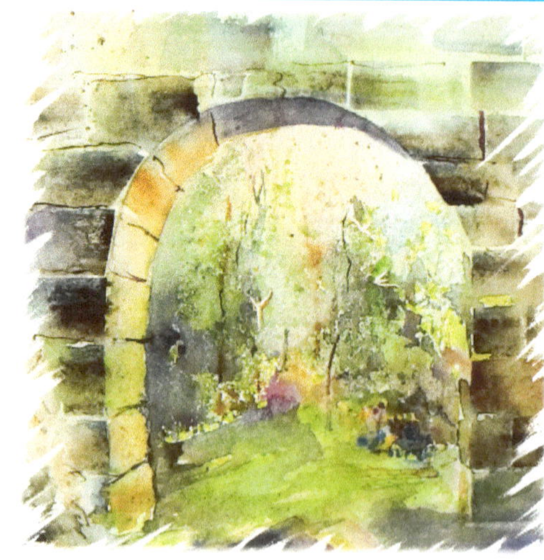

Nymphs

Brown skinned nymphs with dark
eyes
that glisten in reflected light
pass through the mist-shrouded
archway
erected with large rectangular
stones
glowing a dull dark color
the garden
which lies beyond sends fragrant
bouquets
of luscious scents across our
nostrils
until we all sneeze with excitement
the energy rushing between us
unable
to be controlled or contained
an arc
of lightning leaps not from the
heavens
but from wet shiny skin to another
and another till all the forty seven
nymphs
are become transparent with pink
webs of
veins below the surface of onion-
like skin
and the smell of the place becomes
pregnant
with a delicious perfume
and all the forms
suddenly become entangled
hugging and kissing
and writhing around on grass so
soft
you were never sure if it was
touching you
or you only imagined contact
as when you reach your hand
through a mirage
that you were sure must be as real
as your most personal beliefs
and as easily exchanged
for something different
until the silence could no longer
encase the activity
which wrapped around our eyelids
prying them open so we must at
last really look
at one another
and cry with the most blessed relief
to see images of ourselves
not some hoary monstrous
appearance
and afterwards there is a rest so
peaceful
that just one instant renews our
strength
for a thousand centuries and as
many lifetimes of activity
during which we accomplish only
to return home

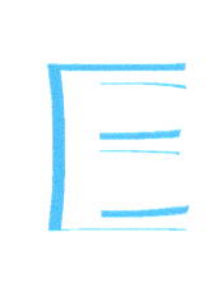

No Path

Lover, oh lover how you transport me
Revealing along the way
Parts of myself long hidden away
The trail is lost
No one has gone this way before
There is no path to follow
And just when I feel hopelessly
Lost, vulnerable, trembling with fear
Longing for comfort, safety
Some familiar sign that is recognizable
Just at that moment of panic and terror
The light becomes so bright
That all shapes disappear and I
Also disappear and there are no
Remaining questions, uncertainties,
doubts,
Desires, conquests or losses
There is only awareness
Without beginning, without end
Oh joy, oh joy, oh beyond joy
There is such beauty
Such saturated richness
Oh, my God!

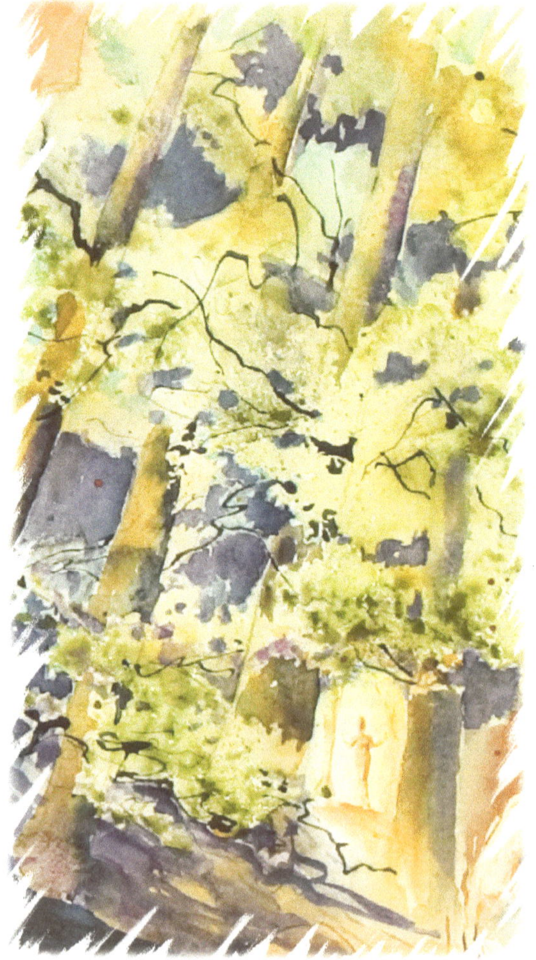

Afterword

Written to each other over a period of fifteen years, these erotic words of love present our personal testimony that couples can create and sustain passionate monogamy. Our lust is an enchantment, a key unlocking a door into the great mystery. Our commitment is a gift, given and received, never a duty, sacrifice or obligation. Through our shared belief that body, mind, heart, and soul are one, that sex and spirit belong together, we offer our love in service to God and Goddess. We try to set the best example we can of how one couple celebrates the Divine by loving each other.

In our early days together, our lovemaking was primarily ***friction sex* -** hungry bodies rubbing together. Friction sex is lusty, panty-wetting and trouser-tenting, a very physical aching for release. Over the years, with sacred sexuality practices, our lovemaking expanded to embrace not only lusty friction but also powerful emotional and spiritual interchange. Friction sex ripened into energy sex. Energy sex evolved into soul sex.

While bestowing extraordinary physical pleasure, ***energy sex*** goes far beyond the physical. Hearts open fully in vulnerable surrender to each other. The deep emotional connection of energy sex paves the way to sexual ecstasy, wherein we *become* the lovemaking. Energy bodies and auras merge in a union of sexual bliss. We may wonder, "Whose orgasm is it anyway?"

From energy sex our sacred lovemaking awakened into ***soul sex***. Letting go of control, we are utterly transparent, open to one another and to the Divine. We invite the sacred spirit out to play. Emotionally naked, physically satiated, reverent and joyous, we unite mystically with the All ~ the most profound love imaginable.

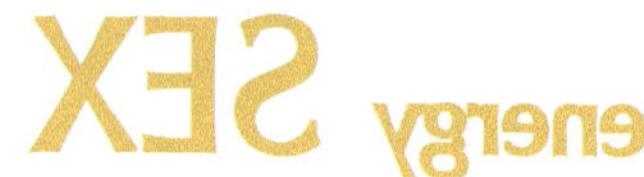

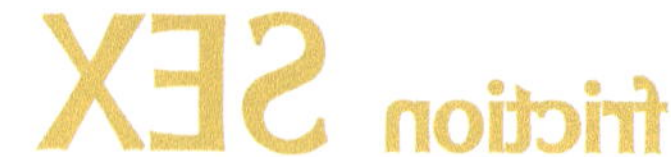

About the Authors

Pala Copeland and Al Link have been practicing Tantric sex since 1987 and teaching sacred sex and conscious relationship since 1997. Their other books include: *The Complete Idiot's Guide to Supercharged Kama Sutra; Sensual Love Secrets for Couples: The Four Freedoms of Body, Mind, Heart & Soul; Soul Sex: Tantra for Two; 28 Days to Ecstasy for Couples: Tantra Step by Step*. They have been featured on the Discovery Channel, Life Channel, Life Network, Women's Television Network, Playboy Radio, Wall Street Journal, Redbook, Ladies Home Journal, Cosmopolitan and many others.
Visit their website: http://www.tantra-sex.com

About the Artist

Val Bradley, a watercolour artist for twenty-five years, enjoys a prosperous full-time career in painting. Her art graces personal, corporate, and public collections throughout North America. Prints and original works can be viewed and ordered at her website: http://www.valbradleywatercolours.com

Book Design

Conceived, edited, and executed by **Gail Marion**
Reformatted by **Reema Sehgal**

ISBN 978-0-9965565-0-7

www.ingramcontent.com/pod-product-compliance
Lightning Source LLC
LaVergne TN
LVHW070145110826
845147LV00002B/329
9780996556507